easy fish & seafood

Delphine de Montalier

easy fish & seafood

whole fish, fish fillets, shellfish and crustaceans

photographs by David Japy

HACHETTE
Illustrated

Buying fish

with confidence!

freshly caught

fresh fish

Tips for buying fish

Whether you buy your fish from a well-patronized fishmonger or a well-stocked supermarket, make sure their selection is as fresh as possible.

Fresh fish should always be displayed on a deep bed of clean ice, and the labels should never be stuck into the flesh. If they won't let you smell the fish, don't buy it.

Whole fish or fish fillets?

Buy whole fish when it's available as it's easier to tell how fresh it is. It's also often cheaper than fillets and you can use the trimmings to make a fish stock.

Fresh fish

• fresh fish should always smell of the sea, with just a hint of seaweed;
• the gills should be red (or pink) and shiny indicating the presence of oxygen, and should not smell (gills stay red for up to four days);
• the eyes should be shiny, never opaque, with black pupils;
• the flesh should be firm to the touch and regain its shape when the pressure is released.

Buying with confidence

Once you have chosen your fish, ask the fishmonger to scale, gut and fillet it for you. He knows what he's doing and his equipment will certainly be better than yours.

Choosing fillets

Buying fillets is really easy – they should have a fresh, light smell and be translucent rather than opaque. The edges should never be dry or discoloured with a yellow or reddish tinge. The flesh should be firm and the skin shiny.

One last tip

First choose fish that is as fresh as possible and offers the best value for money, then think about what you are going to do with it.

How much do you buy?

Allow the following amounts per person:
• fish steaks or fillets: 200 g/7 oz
• fish portions: 250 g/8 oz
• whole fish: 350 g/11½ oz
• smoked fish: 100 g/3½ oz
• raw fish: 100 g/3½ oz

Preparing fish

If your fishmonger hasn't already scaled, trimmed, gutted and filleted the fish for you, then it's up to you to do it.

Scaling

Use a scaler and work your way from the tail to the head. If you haven't got a scaler, then scrape vigorously with the blade of a kitchen knife.

Note: don't remove the scales if the fish is going to be grilled (broiled) or cooked on the barbecue.

Trimming

Remove the head with a large kitchen knife, cut off the fins with a sharp pair of kitchen scissors and then rinse the fish well before you gut it.

Gutting

Use a sharp pair of kitchen scissors or a very sharp kitchen knife to make a slit along the underside of the fish, starting from the opening near the gills. Remove the entrails and the black membrane adhering to the stomach, then rinse the fish again.

Filleting

This technique applies to flat fish, such as sole. Using a knife with a long, slender and well-sharpened blade, make an incision along the backbone from the head to the tail. Insert the blade carefully under the flesh and slide it along the bones towards the tail. Carefully remove the fillets from the centre outwards and from the head the to tail.

Removing the skin from a fillet

Place the fish fillet flat, skin side down, on the work surface (counter) and cut through the tail to the skin. Slide the blade of the knife between the flesh and the skin, holding the tail firmly between your fingers.

Removing the bones

Use a pair of tweezers to remove the bones. For those that prove more difficult, thread the bone through the blade of a paring knife, twist and pull and it should come away.

Keeping fish

Fish goes off quickly and needs to be cooked soon after being bought — after a day or two, it will be far from fresh.

Remove the fish from its wrapping, rinse and blot dry with kitchen paper (paper towels). Wrap carefully in kitchen foil or place on a dish and cover with clingfilm (plastic wrap) and store on the top shelf of the refrigerator.

Cooked fish

Cooked fish will keep for 2–3 days in an airtight plastic container in the centre of the refrigerator.

Freezing fish

You can also freeze fish for up to 6 months at a constant temperature of -18°C/-0.4°F.

Before freezing a whole fish, it's a good idea to coat it with oil before wrapping it carefully in kitchen foil. This way the scales and skin don't 'cook' on contact with the cold and it will still look fresh when it's thawed.

A good way to freeze fillets is to wrap them in clingfilm (plastic wrap) and store in individual bags. It's also a good idea to label the bags since, after a few months, you'll probably have forgotten whether it's hake or cod.

Thawing fish

Place the fish on the bottom shelf of the refrigerator so that it thaws slowly.

Leave whole fish — 1.5–2 kg/3 lb–4 lb — for 24 hours. Fillets will take 6–8 hours.

If you really can't wait that long, you can speed up the process by thawing the fish in the microwave, steaming it or cooking it in stock.

When cooking a frozen fish, remember to almost double the cooking time.

Note: thawed fish should be eaten the same day.

Handy hint

Why not keep a bag of uncooked fish pieces in the freezer that can be used to make a quick lunch or supper for the kids? That way you don't have to rush out to the fishmonger or supermarket to give them fresh fish.

Cooking fish

* Fish doesn't take long to cook and it loses its flavour and dries out if overcooked, which is a real pity.

* Cooking times depend on a number of different factors (type and cut of fish, fat content, cooking method), so it's really a matter of learning to judge when fish is cooked.

* When the flesh becomes opaque, you'll know the fish is cooked.

* Choose the cooking method that best suits the presentation and cut of the fish – whole, in portions, steaks or fillets.

* The best way to cook large fish whole is in an aromatic stock or in the oven (roast or braised).

* Fish portions and fillets (or steaks) are best cooked in foil, steamed, pan-fried, grilled (broiled) or cooked on the barbecue.

Cooking in a court-bouillon

Cooking fish in a court-bouillon – an aromatic stock made from fish stock or water – not only means there is less in the way of cooking smells, but it is also much healthier. Ideally you need a fish kettle but, if you don't have one, you can use a roasting tin (pan) lined with a piece of muslin (cheesecloth). Make sure the edges come over the rim of the pan. This enables you to remove the fish in one piece.
Place the fish in the kettle with the cold stock but don't 'drown' it – the stock needs to be thick, well seasoned and slightly sharp. Heat, uncovered, until the stock simmers gently – don't let it boil. When the fish is cooked, remove the pan from the heat but leave the fish in the stock. This way it will stay warm, without continuing to cook, until you are ready to serve it.

The cooking times suggested here are only intended as a guide, so check the fish at regular intervals and don't leave it unattended.
The cooking time starts when the stock has begun to simmer.

A few cooking times
- Bass (2 kg/4 lb): 10 minutes
- Cod (2 kg/4 lb): 30 minutes
- Sole (500 g/1 lb): 5 minutes
- Conger eel (middle body) (2 kg/4 lb): 20 minutes
- Hake (2 kg/4 lb): 15 minutes
- Mullet or snapper (2 kg/4 lb): 15 minutes

Classic court-bouillon

Preparation: 10 minutes
Cooking: 40 minutes
For 1 kg/2 lb fish

2 litres/3½ pints/8¾ cups water
2 onions, each stuck with 1 clove
2 tablespoons lemon juice
2 tablespoons white wine vinegar
1 thyme sprig
1 fennel sprig
1 bay leaf
2 tablespoons coarse salt
1 tablespoon black peppercorns, in a muslin (cheesecloth) bag

Put all the ingredients into a large pan, bring to the boil and simmer over a medium heat for 30 minutes. Remove the peppercorns and continue cooking for another 10 minutes. Remove the pan from the heat and leave the stock to stand for 1 hour before straining.

Spicy court-bouillon

2 litres/3½ pints/8¾ cups water
2 tablespoons lemon juice
1 tablespoon white wine vinegar
5 bird's eye chillies
4 slices fresh root ginger
rind of 1 orange
1 star anise
1 tablespoon coriander seeds
1 tablespoon fennel seeds
1 clove
1 thyme sprig
1 bay leaf
2 tablespoons coarse salt
1 tablespoon black peppercorns, in a muslin (cheesecloth) bag

Method as for classic court-bouillon.

Court-bouillon with (hard) cider

1 litre/1¾ pints/4¼ cups water
1 litre/1¾ pints/4¼ cups dry (hard) cider
1 onion, peeled and stuck with a clove
1 carrot, coarsely chopped
1 leek, coarsely chopped
1 celery stick (stalk), coarsely chopped
8 parsley sprigs
2 tablespoons coarse salt
1 tablespoon black peppercorns, in a muslin (cheesecloth) bag

Method as for classic court-bouillon.

Variation • you can use dry white wine instead of (hard) cider, in which case, use 500 ml/17 fl oz/generous 2 cups wine along with 1.5 litres/2½ pints/6 cups water.

'Fumet' or aromatic fish stock

Preparation: 5 minutes
Cooking: 15 minutes

500 g/1 lb white fish heads (gills removed) and trimmings
2 litres/3½ pints/8¾ cups water
2 carrots
1 leek
2 shallots
2 tablespoons white wine vinegar
2 tablespoons lemon juice

Put all the ingredients into a large pan, bring to the boil and simmer over a medium heat for 15 minutes. Strain and leave to cool.

Note • A 'fumet' is a more concentrated form of court-bouillon made with fish heads and trimmings left over after the fish has been filleted, or obtained from your fishmonger. A 'fumet' can be used as the basis for a soup or as a stock for poaching fish fillets by simmering gently for a few minutes.

Cooking in the oven

Grilled (broiled) fish

When grilling (broiling) fish, take its thickness into account when positioning it under the grill (broiler) – the thicker the fish, the further it should be from the heat, otherwise it won't cook properly. For successful results, line the grill (broiler) pan with a sheet of foil and place the fish in the pan. Season with salt and pepper, place it under the grill (broiler) and keep an eye on it. About two-thirds of the way through the recommended cooking time, when the skin blackens and blisters, remove the pan and peel off the skin. Turn the fish over and place on a fresh piece of foil. Replace the pan back under the grill (broiler).

This method is worth the extra effort as it allows the fish to cook properly and prevents the cooked flesh lying in a mixture of cooking juices and grilled (broiled) skin. It can be used for all kinds of fish which can be flavoured with olive oil or butter and/or stuffed with fennel, coriander (cilantro) or even tapenade (a purée from southern France made with pitted black olives, capers, anchovies, herbs, olive oil and lemon juice).

The cooking times given here are only intended as a guide, so keep your eye on the fish and keep testing to see if it is cooked.

A few cooking times
• Turbot (1.25 kg/2½ lb): 15 + 5 minutes
• Bass (1.5 kg/3 lb): 9 + 5 minutes
• Bass (500 g/1 lb): 7 + 3 minutes
• Mackerel: 7 + 3 minutes
• Sardines: 5 + 3 minutes
• Sea bream (porgy) (2 kg/4 lb): 15 + 7 minutes
• John Dory (1.25 kg/2½ lb): 8 + 5 minutes
• Red mullet (red snapper): 7 + 3 minutes

Fish in a salt crust

This method involves cooking the fish in a thick coating of coarse salt mixed with egg white (1 kg/ 2 lb salt for 2 egg whites) and leaving it to stand for a few minutes in its crust before serving. One very important thing to remember is that you should not scale the fish before cooking it. Cooking fish in a salt crust is recommended for good-quality fish with flesh that is delicate and not too dense, like bass or sea bream (porgy,) for example.

A few cooking times
• Fresh haddock, bass (1 kg/2 lb): 30 minutes
• Sea bream (porgy) (1.25 kg/2½ lb): 30 minutes
• Bass (2 kg/4 lb): 45 minutes
• Mullet (snapper) (2 kg/4 lb): 35 minutes

Braised fish

Braising can be used for whole fish or fish portions but, either way, the fish is cooked in an ovenproof dish with a lid. The dish can be lined with vegetables but you must remember to moisten the contents with white wine or stock at regular intervals. Stuffings can be varied according to what you have to hand and/or which produce is in season. This method is an excellent way of cooking sea bream (porgy), halibut or plaice (flounder), and even small fish such as red mullet (red snapper) stuffed with tapenade.

A few cooking times
• John Dory (1.5 kg/3 lb): 30 minutes
• Sea bream (porgy) (1 kg/2 lb): 20 minutes
• Plaice (flounder) (750 g/1½ lb): 20 minutes
• Turbot (2 kg/4 lb): 40 minutes
• Red mullet (red snapper): 15 minutes for larger fish, 7–10 minutes for smaller ones
• Monkfish (angler fish) tail (2 kg/4 lb): 30 minutes

Fish cooked in foil

This is an easy way to cook fish and reduces unpleasant smells. First season the fish with olive oil, lemon or thyme – or even tomatoes, olives, vanilla or ginger – then seal it in a double layer of cooking foil or greaseproof (waxed) paper. It is a very quick method and ideal for fillets, fish portions and small fish – but you do need to know your oven in order to adapt the cooking times. You can flavour the fish with spices, herbs and vegetables but don't be too heavy handed as it's a method that concentrates the flavours.

A few cooking times
• Cod steaks (200 g/7 oz): 20 minutes
• Pollack steaks (175 g/6 oz): 15 minutes
• Salmon steaks (200 g/7 oz): 20 minutes
• Red mullet (red snapper): 20 minutes for larger fish, 10 minutes for smaller ones.
• John Dory fillets (150 g/5 oz): 12 minutes
• Fillets of young halibut (160 g/5½ oz): 10 minutes
• Hake steaks (175 g/6 oz): 15 minutes

Cooking in a steamer

This is an ideal way to cook steaks cut from firm-fleshed fish.

Bring an aromatic stock to the boil and place the fish steaks on a bed of lettuce leaves in the perforated container or basket of the steamer (the leaves will protect the fish).
Cover the steamer and allow 3–10 minutes, depending on the thickness of the steaks.

Use the steamer on a low heat for more delicate fish. If you don't have a metal or bamboo steamer, you can steam the fish between two plates over a pan of boiling water.

You can also use a colander, but make sure the fish doesn't come into contact with the stock and extend the cooking time by 2–3 minutes.

Always check to make sure the fish is properly cooked – it is ready when the flesh has a pearly sheen both inside and out and when the 'flakes' begin to separate of their own accord. It is overcooked if the flesh begins to break up.

The best way to check whether fish is properly cooked is to touch it. It should be firm yet soft to the touch and not crumble under pressure.

Place the fish on a bed of lettuce leaves or coat the surface of the steamer, colander or plate liberally with olive oil to prevent the fish from sticking during cooking.

Seaweed, lemon slices, thyme and bay leaves are all flavourings that are associated with steamed fish. They can be added to the stock or placed under the fish.

A few cooking times
- Sole fillets (150 g/5 oz): 2–3 minutes
- Whiting portions (200 g/7 oz): 5–6 minutes
- Red mullet (red snapper) (200 g/7 oz): 5–8 minutes
- Red mullet (red snapper) fillets (100 g/3½ oz): 2–3 minutes
- Grouper fillets (175 g/6 oz): 5–6 minutes
- Pollack fillets (200 g/7 oz): 5–6 minutes
- Cod steaks: 7–10 minutes
- Pollack steaks (175 g/6 oz): 5–7 minutes

Cooking in the microwave

This is a really simple way to cook fish fillets. Put the fillets in a microwave-safe dish, folding the tail ends under so that the fish is the same thickness all over, season and cover with microwave-safe cling-film (plastic wrap). Set the timer. Leave the fish to stand for a few minutes before serving.

A few cooking times
- Haddock fillets (175 g/6 oz): 5 minutes
- Cod fillets (200 g/7 oz): 6 minutes
- Plaice (flounder) fillets (175 g/6 oz): 5 minutes
- Sole fillets (200 g/7 oz): 3 minutes

Pan-frying, grilling (broiling) and cooking in breadcrumbs

For small pieces of fish, coat in flour and fry in an oiled frying pan (skillet). For larger pieces or fillets with skin, brush with a little olive oil and seal over a high heat to form a crisp coating and then finish cooking over a medium heat. Season with salt half-way through cooking so that the fish doesn't stick to the pan.

If you prefer to use butter rather than olive oil, make sure it doesn't burn – not only does it spoil the taste, it's also really unhealthy.

A few cooking times
• Sole portions (250 g/8 oz): in butter, 3 minutes on each side
• Tuna steaks (200 g/7 oz): in butter, 2 minutes on each side for rare steaks
• Monkfish portions (100 g/3½ oz): lightly brown in olive oil on all sides for 3 minutes
• John Dory fillets (150 g/5 oz): in olive oil, skin side only for 5 minutes; cover to finish cooking once sealed
• Cod steaks (200 g/7 oz): in olive oil, skin side only for 5 minutes; cover to finish cooking once sealed
• Salmon steaks (200 g/7 oz): in olive oil, skin side only for 10 minutes; cover to finish cooking once sealed

Fish in breadcrumbs

You can also coat fish in breadcrumbs before cooking – your kids will love it! Roll the fish in flour, dip in beaten egg and then coat with breadcrumbs. Don't do this too far in advance or the coating will crack and dry out. The process can be varied by brushing the fish pieces with mustard before applying the breadcrumb mixture.

Traditional breadcrumbs
Roll the fish fillets in flour, dip in beaten egg and coat with breadcrumbs before frying in butter or olive oil.

Spicy breadcrumbs
The method is the same as above; just simply add spices to the breadcrumbs according to taste – ground cumin, mixed spices (pepper, nutmeg, cloves and cinnamon) or mild chilli powder. But don't be too heavy handed or you'll spoil the flavour of the fish.
Fish coated in breadcrumbs goes well with lemon, so serve with lemon wedges.

Deep-frying

Heat the oil to 180–190°C (350–375°F), or until a cube of bread browns in 30 seconds. Plunge the fish into the hot oil. If you don't have a deep-fryer, you can use a wok. However, a word of advice – if you don't have an extractor, avoid this method of cooking fish.

Deep-frying is ideal for small fish and fish pieces. Thick portions of fish don't cook through on the inside, even though they have a nice crisp coating. Before frying the fish, pat dry with kitchen paper (paper towels) and coat with flour and breadcrumbs or batter. Deep-fried fish cooks very quickly, so keep an eye on it. When it's cooked, drain on kitchen paper (paper towels).

It's impossible to give cooking times, you just have to stand over it and taste to see if it's ready – but take care, it'll be very hot. Small fish are cooked when they are nice and golden with a crisp coating.

Tempura batter

FOR 30 SMALL PIECES OF FISH
2 egg yolks
250 ml/8 fl oz/1 cup iced water
65 g/2½ oz/⅔ cup plain (all-purpose) flour
150 g/5 oz/⅔ cup cornflour (cornstarch)
1.5 litres/2½ pints grapeseed oil

Beat the egg yolks with the measured iced water in a bowl. Combine the flour and cornflour (cornstarch) in another bowl, pour in the beaten egg mixture and mix together – don't worry if there are a few lumps. Heat the oil in a deep-fryer or wok.
Dip the fish pieces in the batter and fry in small batches for about 2 minutes until they are crisp and golden.

Cooking on the barbecue

There's nothing like cooking outdoors – it's practical and there's no lingering smell in the house.

It's best to use a double grill as this enables you to turn the fish easily – make sure it is absolutely clean and well oiled.

Wait until the flames have died down on your barbecue and the charcoal is nice and hot.

The distance of the fish from the embers should vary in relation to its size – 10–12 cm/4–5 inches for small fish and fish slices, 15–20 cm/6–8 inches for larger pieces.

For successful barbecuing (grilling), choose medium-thick cuts of fish that will cook evenly – slices and pieces that are not too thick, fillets that are not too thin (remembering to moisten them with wine or stock at regular intervals) and small whole fish. If you use larger fish, score them diagonally for better heat distribution.

Whether you use whole fish, fish fillets or fish kebabs, you can marinate them in the refrigerator for a few hours before barbecuing (grilling).

**A few cooking times
(a rough guide)**
• Red mullet (red snapper): 7–8 minutes for small fish; 10–12 minutes for larger ones
• Mackerel: 7–8 minutes for small fish; 10–12 minutes for larger ones
• Sardines: 6–7 minutes, depending on their size
• Fish slices (about 3 cm/1¼ inches thick): 8–10 minutes
• Whole fish (1 kg/2 lb–1.5 kg/3 lb): 15–20 minutes

Asian marinade

**100 ml/3½ fl oz olive oil
2-cm/¾-inch piece of fresh root ginger, grated
pinch saffron powder
grated rind ½ unwaxed lemon**

Mix together all the ingredients and pour over the fish. Leave to marinate in the refrigerator for at least 30 minutes. This marinade is ideal for salmon, tuna and sea bream (porgy).

Aphrodisiac marinade

**4 tablespoons lemon juice
1 fresh chilli, deseeded and thinly sliced
2 tablespoons soy sauce
2 pinches ground ginger
2 chives, chopped**

Mix together all the ingredients and pour over the fish. Leave to marinate for at least 3 hours – ideal for salmon, tuna and swordfish.

Wine marinade

**2 tablespoons soy sauce
150 ml/¼ pint/⅔ cup sweet white wine
2 tablespoons sugar
3 tablespoons olive oil
½ bunch of coriander (cilantro), finely chopped
1 tablespoon pink peppercorns**

Mix together all the ingredients and pour over the fish. Leave to marinate for 20 minutes – ideal for cod, haddock, salmon and hake.

Spicy marinade

**3 garlic cloves, finely chopped
2 tablespoons lemon juice
200 ml/7 fl oz/scant 1 cup dry white wine
1 tablespoon flat leaf parsley, chopped
dash of Tabasco sauce**

Mix together all the ingredients and pour over the fish. Leave to marinate for 1 hour – ideal for tuna, salmon, cod and sea bream (porgy).

Serving fish

Whole fish, whether cooked in the oven or poached in stock, can sometimes look unappetizing. It's often better to prepare fillets than serve a whole fish with opaque eyes and bones in the flesh that are more likely to put your guests off their food than make them want a second helping.

Is it properly cooked?

Before serving fish, always check that it is properly cooked – the head should be easy to remove, there should be the slightest hint of pink near the backbone and the fillets should come away easily from the bones. The flesh should have a pearly sheen or be very white (depending on the fish) and slightly firm and soft to the touch.

Before serving

Remove the skin, take out the bones along the side and cut two fillets. Turn the fish over and do the same on the other side.
Check that there are no bones left and serve the fish on a warm dish.

Serving on a warm dish

There are several ways to prepare a warm serving dish: stand it in the sink and pour boiling water over it just before serving; stand it in the sink and run the hot tap (faucet); heat it in the oven on its lowest setting; fill it with water and heat it in the microwave. Any of these methods will make sure that your fish is served piping hot.

Draining fish

Before serving fish cooked in stock, make sure it has been well drained on kitchen paper (paper towels) before placing it on the serving dish or serving on individual plates.
Fried fish should also be drained on kitchen paper (paper towels) before being served.

Ready to serve

If your fish is cooked and ready to serve and your guests are lingering over their pre-dinner drinks, don't panic. Simply cover the fish with foil and place in a preheated oven, 150°C (300°F), gas mark 2, leaving the door slightly ajar. Use the time to run the plates under hot water.

Which wine?

Grilled (broiled) fish and fish cooked in stock not only goes well with dry white wines, such as Chablis, Pouilly Fumé, Pouilly-Fuissé, Sancerre and Muscadet, but also velvety wines that are neither too dry nor too sweet – Montrachet, Meursault, dry Vouvray, Riesling – and even a light red Bordeaux.
Fish cooked in sauce should be accompanied by the wine used in its preparation.
Always serve shellfish with very dry white wines.

On the table

A good quality olive oil and lemon wedges are essential.
There should also be a pepper mill containing black peppercorns only – not a complicated array of mixed spices, and certainly not cloves, which are overpowering and spoil the taste of the fish– and don't forget the sea salt.
If you have them, fish knives and forks add that final touch and are pleasant to use. If you don't, see if you can pick some up from a second-hand shop – they may not match but a white linen tablecloth and a vase of flowers will set them off a treat.

Appetizers

dried roe

anchovy stuffed aubergines
(eggplant)

taramasalata

grilled (broiled)
herring roes

salt cod fritters ...

Dried roe with olive oil and lemon juice

Serves 6–8
Preparation: 10 minutes

6 slices fresh rustic bread, toasted
olive oil, for drizzling
2 dried grey mullet or tuna roes
4 tablespoons lemon juice
freshly ground black pepper
To serve: lemon wedges,

Cut each slice of toast into 3 pieces, arrange on a large serving dish and drizzle with olive oil.
Using a paring knife, cover each piece of toast with thin strips of roe, sprinkle with lemon juice and top with a grinding of pepper.
Serve with lemon wedges.

Tricks of the trade • Dried grey mullet roe is available from some French and Italian delicatessens. Dried tuna roe is mainly a Sicilian speciality. Both are known as poutargue in French and bottarga in Italian.

Open sardine sandwiches

Serves 4
Preparation: 15 minutes

12 canned sardines in oil
4 tablespoons lemon juice
25 g/1 oz/2 tablespoons butter, softened
½ bunch of flat leaf parsley, coarsely chopped
1 fresh crusty baguette
freshly ground black pepper

Drain the sardines, slit them and remove the bones. Mash the flesh with a fork, gradually incorporating the lemon juice, softened butter and chopped parsley. Season with pepper.
Cut the baguette into 4 pieces, then cut each section in half lengthways and remove part of the soft centre. Spread the sardine mixture on each piece of bread and enjoy!

Homemade taramasalata

Serves 6–8
Preparation: 15 minutes

300 g/10 oz smoked cod's roe
2 tablespoons sunflower oil
2 tablespoons lemon juice
2 tablespoons crème fraîche or natural (plain) yogurt
freshly ground black pepper
To serve: toasted fresh rustic bread and lemon wedges

Remove the skin from the cod's roe and discard. Mash the roe with a fork in a large bowl, making sure you separate the eggs. Gradually add the sunflower oil until you obtain a smooth consistency – if there are still a few lumps, you can give the mixture a few short, sharp bursts with a hand-held electric whisk or blender but taramasalata is much better prepared by hand.
Mix in the lemon juice and crème fraîche or yogurt and season with pepper. Taste and adjust the seasoning, adding more lemon, crème fraîche or yogurt and/or pepper if necessary.
Chill before serving with strips of toasted rustic bread and lemon wedges.

Tricks of the trade • You will find smoked cod's roe in the chiller cabinets of some supermarkets, Greek delicatessens and at specialist fish suppliers. Make sure they are nice and soft.

Salmon roe with wasabi

Serves 6–8
Preparation: 15 minutes
Cooking: 10 minutes

18 waxy potatoes
100 ml/3½ fl oz/scant ½ cup crème fraîche or natural (plain) yogurt
1 teaspoon wasabi paste
100 g/3½ oz/scant ½ cup salmon roe
salt and freshly ground black pepper
To serve: hot sake

Scrub but do not peel the potatoes and cook in salted boiling water for 10–15 minutes until tender. Drain and leave to cool.
Cut lengthways and remove and discard one-third of each potato. Then, using a teaspoon or melon baller, scoop out the the remaining two-thirds of flesh, taking care not to damage the skins.
Put the potato skins to one side and mash the scooped out potato with a fork.
Beat together the crème fraîche or yogurt, wasabi and a pinch of salt in a bowl, then mix in the mashed potato. Fill each potato skin with the mixture and top with salmon roe. Season with pepper
Serve the potatoes with a glass of hot sake.

Salt cod fritters

Serves 6
Soaking: 12 hours
Preparation: 30 minutes
Cooking: 30 minutes

400 g/13 oz salt cod
1 bay leaf
200 g/7 oz plain/scant 1¾ cups (all-purpose) flour
½ teaspoon baking powder
150 ml/¼ pint/⅔ cup water
1 onion, chopped
2 garlic cloves, finely chopped
4 chives, chopped
2 eggs, separated
⅓ West Indian chilli, deseeded and finely chopped
oil, for frying
To serve: lemon or lime wedges

Soak the cod in cold water for 12 hours, changing the water several times.

Drain the cod, place it in a pan and add sufficient cold water to cover. Add the bay leaf, bring to the boil and simmer gently over a low heat until the cod is cooked (see page 16). Remove the pan from the heat and leave the fish to cool in the cooking liquid. When it has cooled, drain, remove the skin and bones and flake the flesh.

Put the flour into a large bowl, sprinkle in the baking powder and stir in the measured water, onion, garlic, chives and egg yolks. In a separate bowl, beat the egg whites until they form stiff peaks, then fold into the flour mixture together with the cod and chilli.

Heat the oil in a deep frying pan (skillet) or deep-fryer to 170°C (340°F), or until a cube of bread browns in 40 seconds. Use a teaspoon to scoop out small balls of mixture and add carefully to the oil. Deep-fry for about 3 minutes, until the fritters are crisp and golden, then remove from the oil and drain on kitchen paper (paper towels). Serve immediately with lemon or lime wedges.

Tricks of the trade • West Indian or rocotillo chillies look like small Chinese lanterns. They have a fiery flavour, so use them sparingly. Make sure you remove all the seeds and try not to touch them with your fingers once they've been cut.

Cod rillettes

Serves 6–8
Preparation: 25 minutes
Cooking: 30 minutes

**250 g/8 oz fresh white kidney beans or other
white beans, shelled
1 onion, stuck with a clove
250 g/8 oz cod fillet
a few lettuce leaves
2 tablespoons single (light) cream
2 tablespoons olive oil, plus extra for serving
½ bunch of chives, chopped
sea salt and freshly ground black pepper
To serve: toasted rustic bread**

Cook the beans with the onion in salted boiling
water for 30 minutes.
Meanwhile, pour cold water into the lower part of
a steamer and place the cod fillet on the lettuce
leaves in the upper part or basket. Cover and steam
for 10 minutes (start timing when the water begins
to simmer) and then check that the fish is cooked.
It is cooked when the flesh has a pearly sheen inside
and out and when the 'flakes' begin to separate of
their own accord. It is overcooked if the flesh starts
to crumble. Transfer the fish to a plate lined with
kitchen paper (paper towels) and leave to cool.
When the fish is cold, flake it coarsely with your fingers, removing any remaining bones.
Drain the beans, discard the onion and put the
beans into a blender or food processor with the
fish, cream and olive oil. Pulse to a purée, but don't
over-process the mixture – rillettes should have a
coarse, uneven texture.
Scrape the mixture into a serving dish, or individual
ramekins, and sprinkle with chopped chives.
Season with sea salt and freshly ground pepper.
Serve the rillettes with slices of toasted rustic
bread, olive oil for drizzling and extra sea salt
and pepper.

Cod tartlets

Serves 6–8
Preparation: 20 minutes
Cooking: 20 minutes

3 tablespoons olive oil, for brushing
230 g/8 oz ready-made flaky pastry, thawed if frozen
plain (all-purpose flour), for dusting
¼ lemon
4 teaspoons balsamic vinegar
400 g/13 oz cod fillet
a few lettuce leaves
6 chives, chopped
3 tarragon sprigs, chopped
3 coriander (cilantro) sprigs, chopped
3 parsley sprigs, chopped
sea salt and freshly ground black pepper

Line a baking (cookie) sheet with greaseproof (waxed) paper and brush with oil. Roll out the pastry on a lightly floured work surface (counter) and stamp out 18 rounds with a 6-cm/2½-inch pastry cutter. Put the rounds on the prepared baking (cookie) sheet and prick with a fork. Cook in a preheated oven, 240°C (475°F), gas mark 9, for 10 minutes, then remove from the oven but don't switch it off. Leave to cool for a few minutes, then, using a thin-bladed knife, cut each tartlet case (shell) in half horizontally and return to the oven for 2 minutes. Pour cold water into the lower part of a steamer and add the lemon and 1 teaspoon of the vinegar. Place the fish on a bed of lettuce in the basket or in the upper part. Cover and steam for 10 minutes (start timing when the water begins to simmer), then check that the fish is cooked. It is cooked when the flesh has a pearly sheen inside and out and when the 'flakes' begin to separate of their own accord. Transfer the fish to a plate lined with kitchen paper (paper towels) and leave to cool. When it's cold, break into small pieces, removing any remaining bones.
Prepare a vinaigrette by whisking together the remaining vinegar and the olive oil and season with sea salt and pepper. Stack the tartlet cases (shells) together in pairs, drizzle each with vinaigrette and top with pieces of cod and chopped herbs. Finish with a drizzle of vinaigrette on each tartlet.

Crispy tuna and tomato tartlets

Prepare the pastry cases as for the cod tartlets. To make the filling, put 230 g/7½ oz drained, canned, chopped tomatoes, 2 finely chopped garlic cloves, 1 tablespoon sugar and 1 tablespoon olive oil into a pan, season with salt and pepper and cook for 30 minutes over a low heat.
Heat 1 tablespoon olive oil in a frying pan (skillet), add 300 g/10 oz fresh tuna steak and cook over a high heat for 2 minutes on each side. Leave to cool, then cut into 18 thin slices.
Spread the tomato mixture on the tartlet cases (shells), put together in pairs and top with a slice of tuna and a basil leaf. Season with salt and pepper and serve immediately.

Anchovy stuffed aubergines (eggplant)

Serves 6–8
Preparation: 30 minutes
Standing: 20 minutes
Cooking: 40 minutes

4 large aubergines (eggplant)
olive oil, for brushing
30 g/1 oz/½ cup fresh breadcrumbs
100 ml/3½ fl oz/scant ½ cup milk
10 canned anchovy fillets in oil, drained
2 tablespoons crème fraîche or natural (plain) yogurt
4 tablespoons lemon juice
18 sage leaves
salt and freshly ground black pepper

Cut 2 of the aubergines (eggplant) lengthways into 9 slices, each about 5 mm/¼ inch thick. Sprinkle with salt, cover with a clean tea (dish) towel and leave for 20 minutes. Place the 2 whole aubergines (eggplant) under a preheated grill (broiler) turning often, until the skins blister and char. Remove and wrap in foil. Line a baking (cookie) sheet with greaseproof (waxed) paper and brush with oil. Place the aubergine (eggplant) slices on the sheet and brush with olive oil. Add the foil-wrapped aubergines (eggplant) and bake in a preheated oven, 200°C (400°F), gas mark 6, for 15 minutes. Turn the aubergines (eggplant), and brush the slices with more oil. Bake for 15 minutes longer. Meanwhile, soak the breadcrumbs in the milk. Remove the aubergines (eggplant) from the oven, unwrap the whole ones, cut them in half lengthways and leave to cool. Squeeze the excess milk from the breadcrumbs, scoop out the flesh from the aubergine (eggplant) halves and mix with the breadcrumbs, anchovies, crème fraîche or yogurt and lemon juice. Season with pepper.
Place a sage leaf on each aubergine (eggplant) slice, top with a spoonful of filling and roll or wrap up.

Grilled (broiled) herring roes

Serves 4
Preparation: 5 minutes
Cooking: 2 minutes

olive oil, for brushing
250 g/8 oz fresh soft herring roes
4 tablespoons lemon juice
freshly ground black pepper
To serve: toasted baguette slices or crusty bread

Brush a nonstick frying pan (skillet) with oil and heat. Add the roes and cook for 1 minute each side over a high heat. Sprinkle with lemon juice and pepper. Serve hot with the toasted baguette or crusty bread.

Tricks of the trade • Fresh herring roes are available February to March. Some fishmongers sell them separately, others may sell fresh herrings with their roes. Make sure they are really fresh.

Monkfish (angler fish) terrine

Serves 6–8
Preparation: 30 minutes
Cooking: 1 hour 10 minutes

750 g/1½ lb monkfish (angler fish) fillet
8 eggs
3 tablespoons tomato purée (paste)
500 ml/17 fl oz/generous 2 cups crème fraîche
or soured (sour) cream
1 tablespoon Dijon mustard
150 ml/¼ pint/⅔ cup natural (plain) yogurt
½ bunch of chives, chopped
salt and freshly ground black pepper

Steam the fish for 10 minutes (see page 20), then check to see that it's cooked – it should be very lightly done and remain firm. Transfer to a plate lined with on kitchen paper (paper towels) and leave to cool.
Prepare a bain-marie by filling an ovenproof dish or roasting tin (pan) – large enough to accommodate a 25-cm/10-inch rectangular terrine or loaf tin (pan) – with enough water to come two-thirds of the way up the dish. Place it in a preheated oven, 180°C (350°F), gas mark 4.
Beat the eggs in a bowl, then add the tomato purée (paste) and half the crème fraîche or cream. Season with salt and pepper. Cut the fish into chunks about 2 cm/¾ inch thick and add to the egg mixture.
Line the terrine or loaf tin with greaseproof (waxed) paper, pour in the mixture and spread evenly. Cover with the lid or a sheet of foil and cook in the bain-marie for 1 hour (when you put the dish in the oven, the water in the bain-marie should be boiling).
Check that the terrine is cooked by inserting the blade of a kitchen knife – it should come out clean. Leave to cool and then store in the refrigerator until ready to serve.
To make the sauce, mix the remaining crème fraîche with the mustard and yogurt, add the chopped chives and season with salt and pepper.

Tricks of the trade • Monkfish (angler fish) is expensive but the recipe works just as well with cod fillet. If you use cod, you won't need to steam it for quite so long so it's best to keep an eye on it.

Salmon in a sweet-and-sour marinade

Serves 10
Preparation: 10 minutes
Marinating: 9–12 hours

1 salmon, about 1.5–2 kg/3–4 lb
2 kg/4 lb coarse salt
1 kg/2 lb preserving sugar

Ask your fishmonger to cut two salmon fillets, leaving the skin on. Use a pair of tweezers to remove any remaining pin bones.
Mix the salt and sugar together in a large bowl. Place one fillet, skin side down, in a large dish and cover with half the salt and sugar mixture. Place the second fillet on top, skin side down, and cover with the rest of the mixture. Cover with clingfilm (plastic wrap) and leave to marinate in the refrigerator for 9–12 hours. Rinse carefully and pat dry with kitchen paper (paper towels). Using a well-sharpened kitchen knife, remove the skin from the fillets and cut the flesh into small cubes. Serve well chilled, on its own or accompanied by a variety of sauces.

Soy sauce
Mix few spoonfuls of soy sauce with a little wasabi paste and sprinkle with toasted sesame seeds.

Cream sauce with an added extra
Beat 300 ml/½ pint/1¼ cups whipping or double (heavy) cream until thick and flavour with one of the following: grated rind of a lemon or lime, chopped dill or coriander (cilantro), grated fresh root ginger, honey. Whichever flavouring you use, always season with a little pepper.

Variation • You can also serve the salmon in very thin slices. Prepared in this way, the salmon will keep in the refrigerator for up to a week.

Boiled eggs with herring roe

Serves 6
Preparation: 15 minutes
Cooking: 5 minutes

6 eggs
6 slices fresh rustic bread
50 g/2 oz unsalted (sweet) butter
25 g/1 oz hard herring roe

Bring a pan of water to the boil. Using a slotted spoon plunge the eggs into water. Cook for 3 minutes (start timing when the water comes back to the boil), then remove from the pan. While the eggs are cooking, toast and butter the bread and cut into thin strips. Cut the tops off the eggs and add a spoonful of herring roe. Serve in egg cups with toast 'soldiers'.

Whole fish

salmon

mullet

turbot

bass

hake

fresh cod

Mackerel with mustard

Serves 4
Preparation: 5 minutes
Cooking: 7–8 minutes

4 mackerel, gutted and cleaned
oil, for brushing
1 jar strong Dijon mustard, about 200 g/7 oz
1 tablespoon coarse sea salt
3 tablespoons crème fraîche or Greek (strained plain)
yogurt
salt and freshly ground black pepper

Rinse the mackerel under cold running water,
making sure that there are no traces of blood.
Heat the grill (broiler) or light a barbecue. Brush
the rack with oil.
Coat the mackerel with mustard and sprinkle with
coarse sea salt. Place them on the grill (broiler)
rack, put the rack in the pan and place under the
grill (broiler). Alternatively, place them on the grill
rack of the barbecue. Cook for about 5 minutes on
one side, then turn and cook for 2–3 minutes on
the other side.
While the fish is cooking, heat the crème fraîche
or yogurt with 1 tablespoon of the remaining mustard, but do not allow to boil. Season with salt and
pepper. Check that the fish is cooked by pulling away
the backbone at the head end – it should come away
easily.
Serve immediately, accompanied by the warm sauce.

Bass, plain and simple

Serves 6
Preparation: 15 minutes
Cooking: 10 minutes

1 bass, about 2 kg/4 lb, gutted and cleaned
1–2 litres/1³/₄–3¹/₂ pints water
2 bay leaves
4 tablespoons lemon juice
1 tablespoon black peppercorns
1 tablespoon coarse sea salt
To serve: oven-roasted tomatoes with basil (see page 184)
and crushed potatoes (see page 182)

Rinse the cavity of the fish, removing all traces of
black membrane. Put the bass in a fish kettle or
a roasting tin (pan) lined with a piece of muslin
(cheesecloth), making sure that the edges hang
over the rim of the tin (pan) – this will enable you to
remove the fish from the stock in a single piece.
Pour the water into the kettle or roasting tin (pan),
but don't 'drown' the fish, add the bay leaves and
lemon juice and season with salt and pepper.
Gradually bring to the boil, uncovered, skimming off
the scum that rises to the surface. Lower the heat
and simmer very gently for 10 minutes. Do not allow
the stock to come back to the boil. Use a knife to
check that the fish is cooked – the flesh should be
opaque with a pearly sheen, and tinged with pink
near the backbone. Remove from the heat and leave
the fish in its stock until ready to serve.
Serve on a warm dish accompanied by oven-roasted
tomatoes with basil and crushed potatoes.

Variation • You can add spices to the stock or flavour it with
(hard) cider or white wine (see page 16).

Plain cod

Serves 6
Preparation: 15 minutes
Cooking: 20 minutes

1 cod, about 2 kg/4 lb, cleaned and gutted
2–3 litres/3¹/₂–5¹/₄ pints classic court-bouillon
(see page 16)
To serve: crushed potatoes (see page 182)

Prepare the fish as for the bass recipe above.
Put the cod in a fish kettle or roasting tin (pan)
lined with muslin (cheesecloth) and pour in the
court-bouillon, taking care not to 'drown' it.
Cook in the same way as the bass.
Serve immediately on a warm dish accompanied by
a sauce of your choice and crushed potatoes.

Tricks of the trade • You can use this method for cooking all
kinds of fish, just make sure they are fresh. Why not try conger
eel – the middle back is delicious cooked in this way.

Mullet or snapper with green sauce

Serves 6
Preparation: 30 minutes
Cooking: 15 minutes

1 red mullet or red snapper, about 2 kg/4 lb, scaled,
gutted and cleaned
2 litres/3¹/₂ pints classic court-bouillon (see page 16)
4 hard-boiled (hard-cooked) eggs
¹/₃ bunch each chervil, flat leaf parsley, tarragon
and chives, finely chopped
a handful of watercress or rocket (arugula), finely chopped
2 tablespoons white wine vinegar
5 tablespoons olive oil
5 gherkins (dill pickles), drained and chopped
1 tablespoon capers
salt and freshly ground black pepper
To serve: potato salad with shallots

Put the fish in a fish kettle or roasting tin (pan) lined
with muslin (cheesecloth) and add the court-bouillon,
taking care not to 'drown' it. Bring to the boil, lower
the heat and simmer gently for 15 minutes. Remove
from the heat and leave to cool in the stock.
Meanwhile, prepare the green sauce. Shell the eggs
and mash in a bowl. Pour the vinegar and olive oil
into another bowl and season with salt and pepper.
Mix well, then incorporate the mashed eggs, along
with the chopped herbs, watercress or arugula,
gherkins and capers. When the fish has cooled,
remove the fillets and any remaining bones. Pat
dry with kitchen paper (paper towels).
Serve well chilled, accompanied by the green sauce
and a potato salad with shallots.

Cold hake with mayonnaise

Serves 6
Preparation: 10 minutes
Cooking: 5 minutes

1 piece of hake, about 1.25 kg/2¹/₂ lb
1–2 litres/1³/₄–3¹/₂ pints water
1 bay leaf
1 thyme sprig
4 tablespoons lemon juice
1 tablespoon coarse sea salt
1 tablespoon black peppercorns
To serve: mayonnaise (see page 178)

Place the hake in a fish kettle or roasting tin (pan)
lined with a piece of muslin (cheesecloth). Pour in
the water without 'drowning' the fish, add the bay
leaf, thyme and lemon juice and season with salt and
pepper. Without covering, slowly bring to just below
boiling point. As soon as the water begins to bubble,
remove from heat and leave the fish to cool in the
cooking liquid. When cool, peel off the skin, remove
the fillets and pick out any remaining bones with
tweezers. Pat dry with kitchen paper (paper towels)
and chill in the refrigerator until ready to serve.
Serve with a delicious homemade mayonnaise.

Bass in a sorrel crust

Serves 6
Preparation: 20 minutes
Cooking: 25 minutes

1 bass, about 1.5–2 kg/3–4 lb, gutted and cleaned
1½ teaspoons softened butter
2 shallots, finely chopped
2 bunches sorrel or young spinach
1 large ripe tomato, coarsely chopped
6 tablespoons olive oil
sea salt and freshly ground black pepper
To serve: crushed potatoes (see page 182)

Rinse the fish under cold running water and pat dry with kitchen paper (paper towels). Coat the outside with butter, season the cavity with salt and add the shallots.

Rinse the sorrel or spinach, reserving about 12 leaves for the sauce. Blanch the remaining leaves in boiling water for a few seconds and drain. Completely cover the fish with the blanched leaves, wrap in foil and place on a baking (cookie) sheet. Cook in a preheated oven, 220°C (425°F), gas mark 7, for 25 minutes.

Meanwhile, prepare the sauce by processing the reserved leaves, chopped tomato and olive oil in a blender or food processor. Season with sea salt and plenty of pepper.

The fish is cooked when it is still pink near the backbone and when the foil wrapping is swollen and puffy. Carefully remove the foil and sorrel crust — the skin should come away easily at the same time. Remove the fillets and pull out any remaining bones with tweezers.

Transfer to a warm platter and serve immediately, accompanied by the sorrel sauce and crushed potatoes.

Mullet or snapper in a salt crust

Serves 6
Preparation: 15 minutes
Cooking: 35 minutes

1 red mullet or red snapper, about 2 kg/4 lb 8 oz,
gutted and cleaned
4 egg whites
2 kg/4 lb rock salt
2 tablespoons fennel seeds
salt
To serve: olive oil and lemon butter (see page 180)
and spinach

Rinse the fish under cold running water and pat dry with kitchen paper (paper towels). Rub the inside with salt and sprinkle the fennel seeds in the cavity. Mix the egg whites with the rock salt and spread over the base of an ovenproof dish to a depth of about 1.5 cm/3/4 inch thick. Place the fish on top and cover with the remaining rock salt mixture, using your hands to form the crust around the fish and making sure that it is completely enclosed.
Cook in a preheated the oven, 220°C (425°F), gas mark 7, for 35 minutes. Remove from the oven and leave to stand for 10 minutes before breaking the salt crust with a small hammer or cutting it with bread knife. Remove the upper part of the crust and the skin should come away with it.
Serve with olive oil and lemon butter and spinach.

Grilled (broiled) bass with fennel

Serves 6
Preparation: 5 minutes
Cooking: 16 minutes

1 bass, about 1.5 kg/3 lb, or 3 bass, about 500 g/1 lb each,
gutted and cleaned
2 fennel sprigs
1 rosemary sprigs
olive oil, for brushing
sea salt and freshly ground black pepper
To serve: olive oil with fennel seeds (see page 180) and
oven-roasted tomatoes with basil (see page 184)

Rinse the fish under cold running water and pat dry with kitchen paper (paper towels). Season the cavity with salt and pepper and insert the herbs. If you have time, leave to stand to absorb the flavours. Light the barbecue and wait for the flames to die down. Lay the fish on an oiled grill and place about 15–20 cm/6–8 inches above the embers. Alternatively, cook under a preheated grill (broiler). Allow 9 minutes for large fish and 5 minutes for smaller ones.
Turn the fish over and continue cooking for a further 7 minutes for large fish and 3 minutes for smaller ones. When you turn the fish, protect the tail(s) by wrapping in small pieces of foil.

Check that the fish is cooked by pulling away the backbone at the head end – it should come away easily. Peel off the skin and remove the fillets, then pick out as many of the small bones as possible. Serve with olive oil with fennel seeds and oven-roasted tomatoes with basil.

Plaice (flounder) with a hint of sesame

Serves 4
Marinating: 1 hour
Preparation: 5 minutes
Cooking: 20 minutes

2 plaice (flounder), about 750 g/1½ lb each,
gutted and cleaned
4 tablespoons sesame oil
2 tablespoons soy sauce
Tabasco sauce, to taste
2 tablespoons sesame seeds
salt and freshly ground black pepper
To serve: herb salad (see page 184)

Using a sharp knife, make a series of shallow, criss-cross incisions on the upper (dark-skinned) side of the fish.
Mix together the sesame oil, soy sauce and a few drops of Tabasco in an ovenproof dish. Add the fish and marinate in the mixture for 1 hour.
Cook the fish in a preheated oven, at 240°C (475°F), gas mark 9, for 10 minutes, then remove from the oven and check that it is cooked – the flesh should be opaque and white and the fillets should come away easily without breaking up.
While the fish is cooking, warm a serving dish by running it under very hot water.
Dry-fry the sesame seeds in a heavy-based or non-stick pan for a few minutes over a high heat.
To prepare the fish, peel off the skin and remove the fillets from one side. Pull out as many of the small bones as possible. Turn the fish over and remove the other fillets in the same way – each fish provides 2 larger and 2 smaller fillets.
Sprinkle the fillets with toasted sesame seeds, season with salt and pepper and serve immediately with a herb salad.

Monkfish (angler fish) with saffron

Serves 6
Preparation: 15 minutes
Cooking: 30 minutes

2 pinches powdered saffron
200 ml/7 fl oz/scant 1 cup dry white wine
1 preserved lemon
1 monkfish (angler fish) tail, about 1.75 kg–2 kg/3½–4 lb,
skinned and membrane removed
2 garlic cloves, thinly sliced
1 large onion, cut into wedges
4 tablespoons lemon juice
olive oil, for drizzling
To serve: steamed asparagus

Mix the saffron with the white wine in a bowl. Rinse the preserved lemon under cold running water, pat dry with kitchen paper (paper towels) and cut into small pieces. Make small incisions in the fish and insert the slices of garlic.

Line the base of an ovenproof dish with the onion wedges and lemon pieces. Place the fish on top, sprinkle with the lemon juice and pour on the white wine and saffron. Finally, drizzle with olive oil, then cook in a preheated oven, 180°C (350°F), gas mark 4, for 30 minutes, basting frequently with the cooking juices.

Check that the fish is cooked – the flesh should be white inside and out, remaining firm; it shouldn't break up.

When the fish is ready, remove the backbone and cut the tail into several pieces. Place on a warm platter, pour over the cooking juices and serve immediately with steamed asparagus.

John Dory with lime stuffing

Serves 4
Preparation: 15 minutes
Cooking: 30 minutes

**2 John Dory, about 1.25 kg/2½ lb, trimmed, gutted
and cleaned
2 shallots, coarsely chopped
1 garlic clove, coarsely chopped
1 lime, cut into small pieces
½ bunch of coriander (cilantro), plus extra for serving
butter, for greasing
400 ml/14 fl oz/1¾ cups white wine
2 tablespoons olive oil
salt and freshly ground black pepper
To serve: lime wedges**

Make a few well-spaced, shallow incisions on both
sides of each fish.

To prepare the stuffing, process the shallots, garlic,
lime and coriander (cilantro) in a blender or food
processor. Season with salt and pepper.

Fill the cavity with the stuffing, place the fish in a
greased ovenproof dish and pour in the white wine.
Cover with foil and cook in a preheated oven, 180°C
(350°F), gas mark 4, for 30 minutes, basting occasionally with the cooking juices.

Use a small kitchen knife to check that the fish is
cooked – the flesh should be opaque with a pearly
sheen, and tinged with pink near the backbone.

The fillets should come away easily. Remove the fish
and mix the cooking juices with the olive oil.

To prepare the fish for serving, peel off the skin,
remove the fillets and pull out any remaining small
bones with tweezers.

Serve immediately with the sauce, lime wedges and
the extra coriander (cilantro) leaves to garnish.
Green beans with coriander (cilantro) (see page 184)
would make an ideal accompaniment for this dish.

Tuna roast with a spicy crust

Serves 4
Preparation: 10 minutes
Cooking: 12 minutes

1 teaspoon cumin seeds
2 teaspoons fennel seeds
2 teaspoons pink peppercorns
2 teaspoons ground ginger
2 teaspoons ground cinnamon
1 teaspoon coriander seeds
1 teaspoon ground coriander
1 teaspoon freshly grated nutmeg
1 teaspoon lightly crushed black peppercorns
2 tablespoons olive oil, plus extra for brushing
1 tuna fillet, about 875 g/1¾ lb, skinned
2 tablespoons soy sauce
To serve: courgettes (zucchini) sautéed in mixed spices or herb salad (see page 184)

Put all the spices into a blender or spice grinder and process for 5 minutes, until the seeds are properly crushed. Turn out into a bowl.
Brush the tuna fillet with olive oil and coat with the mixed spices. Heat 1 tablespoon of the olive oil in a deep frying pan (skillet) and lightly brown the tuna for 6–8 minutes all over. The spices should form a crisp crust while the fish remains rare inside. If you prefer your fish a little more cooked (pink), cover and continue cooking for 2 minutes. Remove from the pan and keep warm.
Add the soy sauce and remaining olive oil to the pan. Scrape the base and sides to stir in any residue and cook over a low heat for 2 minutes until slightly reduced and thickened. Slice the fish like roast beef and serve immediately with the sauce, accompanied by courgettes (zucchini) sautéed in mixed spices (pepper, nutmeg, cloves and cinnamon) or a herb salad.

Roast turbot or halibut with aromatic oil

Serves 6
Preparation: 10 minutes
Marinating: 1 hour
Cooking: 20 minutes

2 turbot or halibut, about 1.25 kg/2½ lb, trimmed, heads removed, gutted and cleaned
100 ml/3½ fl oz/scant ½ cup olive oil, plus extra for brushing
1 teaspoon ground cumin
1 tablespoon mild chilli powder
To serve: lemon wedges and ratatouille (see page 182), optional

Make a few well-spaced, shallow incisions on the dark-skinned (upper surface) of each fish.
Prepare the marinade by mixing the olive oil and spices in a large dish. Place the fish dark-skinned side down in the dish, cover with clingfilm (plastic wrap) and set aside to marinate for 1 hour in the refrigerator. Preheat the grill (broiler).
Line the grill (broiler) pan with foil and brush with olive oil. Place the fish light-skinned (underside) up, drizzle with 1 tablespoon of marinade and place the pan about 15 cm/6 inches below the heat.
Cook for 15 minutes until the skin chars and blisters. Remove the fish and peel off the skin. Line the grill (broiler) pan with a fresh piece of foil, brush with olive oil and put the fish back in the pan the other way up. Grill (broil) for a further 5 minutes. Use a small kitchen knife to check that the fish is cooked – the flesh should be opaque with a pearly sheen, and tinged with pink along the backbone.
Peel off the remaining skin and remove the fillets. Take out the backbone and as many other bones as possible. Remove the other 2 fillets in the same way Serve the fillets immediately in a hot serving dish, either on their own or with a few lemon wedges and accompanied by ratatouille.

John Dory with spices

Serves 4
Preparation: 15 minutes
Cooking: 15 minutes

1 teaspoon cumin seeds
1 teaspoon fennel seeds
1 teaspoon ground ginger
1 teaspoon ground cinnamon
1 teaspoon coriander seeds
1 teaspoon freshly grated nutmeg
1 teaspoon white peppercorns
olive oil, for brushing and drizzling
2 John Dory, about 1.25 kg/2½ lb, trimmed, heads removed, gutted and cleaned
To serve: braised fennel

Preheat the grill (broiler).
Put all the spices into a blender or spice grinder and process briefly. Brush the fish with olive oil and sprinkle both sides with the mixed spices.
Line the grill (broiler) pan with foil and brush with olive oil. Lay the fish on the foil and place the pan about 15 cm/6 inches below the heat. Cook for 8 minutes, until the skin chars and blisters.
Remove the fish from the grill and peel off the skin. Line the grill (broiler) pan with a fresh piece of foil, brush with olive oil and return the fish back to the pan on the other side. Replace the pan under the grill (broiler) for 5 minutes. Use a small kitchen knife to check that the fish is cooked – the flesh should be opaque with a pearly sheen, and tinged with pink along the backbone. The fillets should come away easily.
Peel off the remaining skin and remove the fillets. Serve immediately with a drizzle of olive oil – plain or flavoured with cumin or mild chilli – and accompanied by braised fennel.

Fillets, steaks and portions

fruity white fish salad

pollack with preserved lemon

red mullet with tapenade

salmon with lemon grass

John Dory fillets with herring roe

cod with lemon thyme...

Fruity white fish salad

Serves 4
Preparation: 15 minutes
Cooking: 5 minutes

350 g/12 oz white fish fillet, such as cod or haddock
2 red onions, cut into small chunks
1 mango, peeled, stoned (pitted) and chopped
4 mint sprigs, chopped
4 coriander (cilantro) sprigs, chopped
2 handfuls of rocket (arugula), chopped
grated rind and juice of 1 lime
3 tablespoons olive oil
1 tablespoon orange juice
salt and freshly ground black pepper

Bring a large pan of water to the boil and poach the fish for 5 minutes over a low heat. Remove the fish from the pan and leave to cool on kitchen paper (paper towels).

Mix together the onions, mango, mint, coriander (cilantro) and rocket (arugula) in a salad bowl. Sprinkle with the lime rind and juice and season with salt and pepper.

As soon as the fish is cold, break it into medium-sized pieces with your fingers and add to the top of the salad.

Prepare a dressing by whisking together the olive oil and orange juice and season with salt and pepper. Pour over the salad and mix carefully.

Serve well chilled.

Variation • You can replace the olive oil with argan oil, which you'll find at fine delicatessen's or North African food stores.

Quick sole fillets

Serves 2
Preparation: 5 minutes
Cooking: 3 minutes

400 g/14 oz sole fillets
200 ml/7 fl oz/scant 1 cup white wine
1 tablespoon crème fraîche or natural (plain) yogurt
a few tarragon leaves, chopped
salt and freshly ground black pepper
To serve: boiled basmati rice

Place the fillets in a microwave-safe dish, folding the tails under so that the fish is the same thickness all over.
Pour over the white wine and season with salt and pepper. Cover with microwave-safe clingfilm (plastic wrap). Place in the microwave and cook for 3 minutes at 750W.
Remove the dish from the microwave and pour off and reserve the cooking juices. Cover the fish and leave to stand. Mix the cooking juices with the crème fraîche or yogurt and chopped tarragon. Serve the sole fillets with the creamy wine and tarragon sauce and boiled basmati rice.

Turbot or halibut with onion mousse

Serves 4
Preparation: 15 minutes
Cooking: 15 minutes

125 g/4 oz/½ cup unsalted (sweet) butter
1 white onion, finely chopped
100 ml/3½ fl oz/scant ½ cup water
olive oil for brushing
8 chicken turbot or chicken halibut fillets
(around 150-200g/5-7 oz)
sea salt and freshly ground black pepper
To serve: steamed potatoes

Reserve 1 tablespoon of the butter and put the remainder in a pan with the onion and measured water. Cook over a low heat for 15 minutes. Meanwhile, cut 16 sheets of foil, each large enough to contain a fish fillet, and put them together in pairs to make a double layer of foil. Brush the top pieces of foil with olive oil. Place a fillet on each foil wrapping, top with a small knob (pat) of the remaining butter and season with salt and pepper. Seal carefully, place the foil parcels on a baking (cookie) sheet and cook in a preheated oven, 220°C (425°F), gas mark 7, for 5 minutes.
When the onion is cooked, process in an blender or food processor. Serve the fish with the onion mousse and steamed potatoes.

Red mullet with tapenade

Serves 4
Preparation: 30 minutes
Cooking: 20 minutes

2 tablespoons olive oil, plus extra for brushing
1 onion, diced
1 red (bell) pepper, deseeded and diced
1 yellow (bell) pepper, deseeded and diced
16 black olives, pitted and chopped
8 medium-sized red mullet or red snapper (heads removed)
salt and freshly ground black pepper
To serve: boiled basmati rice

Heat the olive oil in a deep frying pan (skillet) and cook the onion and (bell) peppers over a high heat for 5–7 minutes, stirring frequently to prevent them from burning. Add the olives and season with salt and pepper.
Cut 16 sheets of foil, each large enough to contain one fish, placing them together in pairs to make a double layer of foil. Brush the top piece of foil with olive oil. Fill each mullet with the vegetable mixture and tie with kitchen string. Place a fish on each wrapping and seal carefully. Put the foil parcels on a baking (cookie) sheet and cook in a preheated oven, 220°C (425°F), gas mark 7, for 10 minutes. Leave the fish in their wrappings so that they are served piping hot. Basmati rice makes an ideal accompaniment for this dish.

Salmon with lemon grass

Serves 4
Preparation: 15 minutes
Cooking: 20 minutes

olive oil, for brushing and drizzling
12 kaffir lime leaves
4 salmon steaks, about 200 g/7 oz each
2 lemon grass stalks, finely chopped
grated rind of 1 lemon
sea salt and freshly ground black pepper
To serve: boiled basmati rice or steamed potatoes

Cut 8 sheets of foil, each large enough to contain a fish steak, placing them together in pairs to make a double layer of foil. Brush the top piece of foil with olive oil. Line each wrapping with 3 lime leaves and place the salmon steaks on top. Sprinkle with chopped lemon grass and grated lemon rind and season with sea salt and pepper. Drizzle with olive oil and seal carefully. Place the foil parcels on a baking (cookie) sheet and cook in a preheated oven, 220°C (425°F), gas mark 7, for 20 minutes.
Remove from the oven and serve the steaks in their foil wrapping so that your guests can enjoy their delicious aroma as they open them.
Of course, you don't eat the lemon grass or lime leaves; they are purely for flavouring. Serve with boiled basmati rice or steamed potatoes.

Foil-wrapped pollack with vanilla cream

Serves 4
Preparation: 10 minutes
Cooking: 15 minutes

40 g/1½ oz/3 tablespoons butter, softened
1 vanilla pod (bean)
olive oil, for brushing
4 pollack fillets, 150–200 g/5–7 oz each
300 ml/½ pint/1¼ cups single (light) cream
salt and freshly ground black pepper
To serve: cardamom rice (see page 186)

Beat the butter in a bowl until thick and creamy. Split the vanilla pod (bean) lengthways, remove the black seeds with the point of a knife and add them to the butter – don't discard the pod. Spread the vanilla butter on the fillets and season with pepper. Cut 8 sheets of foil, each large enough to contain a fish fillet, placing them together in pairs to make a double layer of foil. Brush the top piece of foil with olive oil. Place a fillet on each wrapping and seal carefully. Place the foil parcels on a baking (cookie) sheet and cook in a preheated the oven, 200°C (400°F), gas mark 6, for 12–15 minutes.
While the fish is cooking, pour the cream into a small pan, add the vanilla pod (bean) and season lightly with salt and pepper. Set over a low heat for 10 minutes, strain and keep warm.
Open the parcels, check that the fish is cooked and serve the fillets with the vanilla cream and cardamom rice.

Fillets of John Dory with herring roe

Serves 4
Preparation: 10 minutes
Cooking: 15 minutes

1 tablespoon olive oil, plus extra for brushing and drizzling
4 John Dory fillets, 150–200 g/5–7 oz each, skinned
1 shallot, finely chopped
200 ml/7 fl oz/scant 1 cup single (light) cream
½ bunch of flat leaf parsley, finely chopped
50 g/2 oz hard herring roe
salt and freshly ground black pepper
To serve: steamed green asparagus

Cut 8 sheets of foil, each large enough to contain a fillet, placing them together in pairs to make a double layer of foil. Brush the top piece of foil with olive oil. Place a fillet on each wrapping, drizzle with olive oil and season with salt and pepper. Seal carefully, place the foil parcels on a baking (cookie) sheet and cook in a preheated oven, 220°C (425°F), gas mark 7, for 15 minutes.
Meanwhile, heat a tablespoon of olive oil in a pan, add the chopped shallot and cook over a low heat for 3 minutes, then add the cream and chopped parsley. Season with salt and pepper and heat through for 5 minutes, taking care that it does not boil. Process in a blender until smooth and keep warm.
Remove the fish from the oven and serve on individual plates with a portion of herring roe beside each fillet. Serve with the cream and parsley sauce and steamed green asparagus.

Tricks of the trade • You can buy fresh herring roe from your fishmonger. If he doesn't have any in stock, he may be able to order it for you.

Cod with ginger

Serves 4
Preparation: 15 minutes
Cooking: 20 minutes

olive oil, for brushing and drizzling
3.5-cm/1½-inch piece of fresh root ginger, thinly sliced
4 cod steaks, about 150–200 g/5–7 oz each
8 coriander (cilantro) sprigs
salt and freshly ground black pepper
To serve: herb salad (see page 184)

Cut 8 sheets of foil, each large enough to contain a fish fillet, placing them together in pairs to make a double layer of foil. Brush the top piece with olive oil. Divide the slices of ginger among the wrappings, place the cod steaks on top, sprinkle with coriander (cilantro), drizzle with olive oil and season with salt and pepper. Seal carefully, place the foil parcels on a baking (cookie) sheet and cook in a preheated oven, 220°C (425°F), gas mark 7, for 15 minutes.
Unwrap the parcels and transfer the fish to serving plates, discarding the ginger. Serve immediately accompanied by a herb salad.

Cod with lemon thyme

Serves 4
Preparation: 5 minutes
Cooking: 10 minutes

1 small bunch of lemon thyme
4 cod steaks, about 150–200 g/5–7 oz each
olive oil, for drizzling
sea salt and freshly ground black pepper
To serve: crushed potatoes (see page 182)

Pour cold water into the base of a steamer, line the
upper part with the lemon thyme and place the cod
steaks on top. Cover, bring the water to the boil and
steam for 5 minutes, then tilt the lid to allow some
of the steam to escape and continue cooking for a
further 5 minutes. Check that the fish is cooked
and, if necessary, steam for a further 1–2 minutes.
The fish is cooked when the flesh has a pearly sheen
both inside and out and when the 'flakes' begin to
separate of their own accord. If it is overcooked,
the flesh will begin to break up.
Serve the cod steaks with a drizzle of olive oil, seasoned with sea salt and freshly ground black pepper.
Crushed potatoes make an ideal accompaniment for
this dish.

Red mullet with cherry tomatoes

Serves 4
Preparation: 20 minutes
Cooking: 1 hour 10 minutes

olive oil, for brush and drizzling
4 bunches of cherry tomatoes
1 tablespoon balsamic vinegar
1 teaspoon granulated sugar
1 teaspoon tapenade
2 tablespoons pine nuts
12 mint leaves
16 basil leaves
4 red mullet or red snapper, gutted, cleaned and scaled
sea salt and freshly ground black pepper

Brush an ovenproof dish with olive oil and arrange the bunches of cherry tomatoes in it. Drizzle with olive oil and balsamic vinegar, sprinkle with sugar and season with pepper. Cook in a preheated oven, 110°C (225°F), gas mark ¼, for 1 hour (open the oven door slightly if they show signs of burning). When cooked, wrap in foil and keep warm in the oven. Process the tapenade in a blender with a drizzle of olive oil, the pine nuts, mint and basil leaves. Fill the fish with the mixture.
Pour cold water into the base of a steamer, brush the upper part with oil and place in the fish. Bring the water to the boil and steam the fish for 5–8 minutes, depending on their size.
When the fish are cooked, their colour will soften. Serve with the bunches of roasted cherry tomatoes.

Pollack with preserved lemon

Serves 4
Preparation: 10 minutes
Cooking: 5–7 minutes

olive oil, for brushing
2 preserved lemons, rinsed and cut into 5-mm/¼-inch slices
4 pollack steaks, 180–200 g/6–7 oz each
1 teaspoon mild chilli powder
4 tablespoons argan or pine nut oil
sea salt and freshly ground black pepper
To serve: lemon-braised chicory (Belgian endive; page 182)

Pour cold water into the base of a steamer. When the water begins to boil, brush the upper part with olive oil, line with the lemon slices and top with the pollack steaks. Steam for 5–7 minutes.
When the steaks are cooked remove and keep warm between 2 plates. Coarsely chop the lemon slices and place in a bowl. Sprinkle with chilli powder, add the argan or pine nut oil, season with salt and a little pepper and mix well.
Serve the fish with the lemon sauce and accompanied by lemon-braised chicory (Belgian endive).

Variation • You can also replace the argan oil with olive oil – it's not quite the same but it's still good.

Sea bream (porgy) with seaweed

Serves 4
Preparation: 5 minutes
Cooking: 5 minutes

a handful fresh seaweed, such as kelp, dulse or laver, rinsed
4 sea bream (porgy) fillets, about 200 g/7 oz each
olive oil, for drizzling
sea salt and freshly ground black pepper
To serve: boiled basmati rice

Pour cold water into the base of a steamer and make a bed of seaweed in the upper part. Place the fish on the seaweed, bring the water to the boil and steam for 5 minutes. The fish is cooked when the flesh has a pearly sheen both inside and out and when the flakes begin to separate of their own accord. It is overcooked if the flesh begins to break up.
Serve the fish drizzled with olive oil and seasoned with sea salt and pepper. Basmati rice makes an ideal accompaniment to this dish.

Smoked fish curry

Serves 6
Soaking: 2 hours
Preparation: 20 minutes
Cooking: 30 minutes

875 g/1¾ lb smoked cod or haddock fillets, cut into chunks
1 litre/1¾ pints/4¼ cups milk
2 tomatoes
350 ml/12 fl oz/1½ cups water
2 onions, cut into wedges
2 garlic cloves, crushed
2 tablespoons lemon juice
1 teaspoon curry powder
250 ml/8 fl oz/1 cup canned coconut milk
freshly ground black pepper
15 coriander (cilantro) sprigs, chopped
To serve: boiled basmati rice

Place the fish in a dish, pour in the milk and leave to soak for 2 hours. If necessary, add a little water to ensure the fish is completely covered.
Meanwhile, place the tomatoes in a bowl and cover with boiling water. Leave for 1–2 minutes, drain, cut a cross at the stem end of each tomato and peel off the skins. Coarsely chop the flesh.
Heat the measured water in a pan with the onions, garlic, tomatoes, lemon juice and curry powder. Season with a little pepper, place over a low heat and simmer for 20 minutes. Process in a blender until smooth, then mix in the coconut milk and keep warm. Poach the fish for 3–5 minutes in a large pan of boiling water. Drain, remove the skin and break into large flakes. Put the fish in a large serving dish, add the curry sauce and mix carefully. Sprinkle with chopped coriander (cilantro).
Serve immediately with basmati rice.

Variation • If you don't like coconut milk, use double the amount of water when preparing the curry sauce.

Whiting with lemon grass sauce

Serves 4
Preparation: 5 minutes
Cooking: 15 minutes

2 stems fresh lemon grass
200 ml/7 fl oz/¾ cup single (light) cream
olive oil, for brushing
4 whiting, gutted, cleaned and scaled
1.5-cm/¾-inch piece of fresh root ginger,
cut into thin sticks
2 coriander (cilantro) sprigs, chopped
2 spring onions (scallions), chopped
salt and freshly ground black pepper
To serve: cardamom rice (see page 186)

Remove the lower leaves from the lemon grass, rinse and chop the lower 5 cm/2 inches of the stem finely. Put the cream in a small pan, add the lemon grass and set over a low heat for 15 minutes. Strain, season with salt and pepper and keep warm.
Pour cold water into the base of a steamer and brush the upper part with olive oil. Bring the water to the boil, then place the fish in the upper part of the steamer and sprinkle with the ginger. Cover and steam for 5 minutes.
When the fish is cooked, its colour will soften. Remove the fish from the steamer and carefully remove the fillets from each side.
Place the whiting fillets on serving plates, sprinkle with chopped coriander (cilantro) and spring onions (scallions) and serve with the lemon grass sauce and cardamom rice.

Bass fillets with olive paste

Serves 4
Preparation: 5 minutes
Cooking: 8 minutes

2 pieces of sun-dried tomato in oil, drained
20 black olives, pitted
8 basil leaves
4 tablespoons olive oil
4 bass fillets, about 180 g/6 oz each
freshly ground black pepper
To serve: herb salad (see page 184)

Put the sun-dried tomato, olives, basil leaves and
3 tablespoons of the olive oil into a blender. Season
with pepper and pulse to a thick paste. Spread the
paste over the fish fillets.
Heat the remaining olive oil in a deep frying pan
(skillet) and add the fillets skin-side down. Cook
over a high heat for 3 minutes, keeping them well
separated and gradually reducing the heat – a
crispy skin should form on the base of each fillet.
Cover and continue cooking for 5 minutes over a
low heat.
Serve immediately, accompanied by a herb salad.

Crispy cod

Serves 4
Preparation: 5 minutes
Cooking: 5 minutes

4 cod fillets, about 200 g/7 oz each
2 tablespoons olive oil
salt and freshly ground black pepper
To serve: onion rice (see page 186)

Heat the olive oil in a deep frying pan (skillet) and
add the fish, skin-side down. Cook over a high heat
for 3 minutes, keeping the fillets well separated and
gradually reducing the heat – a crispy skin should
form on the base of each fillet. Season with salt and
pepper, cover and continue cooking for 2 minutes
over a low heat.
Serve immediately, accompanied by the sauce of
your choice and onion rice.

Seared salmon

Serves 4
Preparation: 10 minutes
Cooking: 10 minutes

4 salmon fillets, about 200 g/7 oz each
2 tablespoons lemon juice
6 tablespoons pine nuts
50 ml/2 fl oz olive oil
1 tablespoon balsamic vinegar
sea salt and freshly ground black pepper

Rinse the fish under running water and pat dry
with kitchen paper (paper towels).
Heat a non-stick frying pan (skillet) and add the
fish, skin-side down. Cook over a high heat for
3 minutes, keeping the fillets well separated. Cook
for a further 5 minutes over a medium heat, then
cover and cook for a further 2 minutes.
Meanwhile, put the lemon juice, pine nuts, olive oil
and vinegar into a electric blender or food processor and pulse to combine.
Drain the fish and season with sea salt and pepper.
Serve hot, accompanied by the olive oil and pine
nut sauce.

Sole meunière

Serves 4
Preparation: 5 minutes
Cooking: 6 minutes

4 sole, about 250 g/9 oz each, gutted, cleaned and skinned
2 tablespoons plain (all-purpose) flour
100 g/3½ oz/scant ½ cup butter
4 tablespoons lemon juice
salt and freshly ground black pepper
To serve: steamed potatoes

Rinse the fish under cold running water and pat dry
with kitchen paper. Coat the fish in flour and shake
off any excess.
Melt the butter in a large frying pan (skillet).
When it begins to bubble, lightly brown the sole for
3 minutes on each side, taking care not to let the
butter burn.
Check that the fish is cooked – the flesh should
remain firm but should be easy to detach from the
backbone with the back of a spoon.
Remove the fillets, sprinkle with lemon juice and
season with salt and pepper.
Serve immediately with steamed potatoes.

Tricks of the trade • If you have chosen large sole weighing
500 g/1 lb or more, brown for 5 minutes on each side, then
cover and continue cooking over a low heat until the fillets
come away from the backbone.

Grilled sardines

Serves 6
Preparation: 5 minutes
Cooking: 8–10 minutes

olive oil, for brushing
24 sardines, gutted and cleaned
sea salt and freshly ground black pepper
To serve: lemon or lime wedges, olive oil and
baked potatoes

Lightly brush a preheated cast-iron griddle pan or
the grill of a lighted barbecue with olive oil. Place
the sardines in the pan or on the grill of the barbecue and cook for 5 minutes on the first side. Turn
and cook for 3–5 minutes on the second side.
The fish are cooked when the skin begins to split
and the flesh is opaque.
Season with salt and pepper and serve hot with
lemon or lime wedges and olive oil, accompanied
by baked potatoes.

Tricks of the trade • Grilled sardines are delicious but release
a strong cooking smell. They are best cooked when the weather
is fine and you can use your barbecue.

Rare tuna steaks, Asian style

Serves 4
Preparation: 10 minutes
Cooking: 4 minutes
Marinating: 1 hour

3 tablespoons lime juice
4 tablespoons soy sauce
3 tablespoons olive oil
1.5-cm/3/4-inch piece of fresh root ginger, grated
4 tuna steaks, about 175 g/6 oz each
8 coriander (cilantro) sprigs, chopped
1 tablespoon toasted sesame seeds
freshly ground black pepper
To serve: vermicelli, herb salad (see page 184) or French
(green) beans with coriander (cilantro; see page 184)

Mix together the lime juice, soy sauce, 2 tablespoons
of the olive oil and the grated ginger in a large,
non-metallic dish. Season with pepper.
Place the tuna in the marinade, cover with clingfilm
(plastic wrap) and place in the refrigerator to marinate for at least 1 hour, turning the steaks
2 or 3 times.
Drain the tuna, reserving the marinade. Heat the
remaining olive oil in a deep frying pan (skillet) and
cook the tuna steaks over a high heat for 2 minutes
on each side – the fish should remain red on the
inside. If you prefer it a little more cooked (pink),
cover and continue cooking for 2 minutes.
Keep the steaks warm and pour the reserved marinade into the pan, scraping up the residue on the
base with a wooden spoon. Bring to the boil
and pour over the tuna steaks.
Sprinkle the fish with chopped coriander (cilantro)
and toasted sesame seeds and serve immediately,
accompanied by vermicelli, a herb salad or French
(green) beans with coriander (cilantro).

Monkfish (angler fish), American style

Serves 6
Preparation: 20 minutes
Cooking: 1 hour

**1.25 kg/2½ lb monkfish (angler fish) fillet,
cut into 12 pieces**
3 tablespoons plain (all-purpose) flour
about 5 tablespoons olive oil
3 shallots, thinly sliced
425-g/14-oz can peeled tomatoes
1 small can (about 140 g/4½ oz) tomato purée (paste)
175 ml/6 fl oz/¾ cup white wine
3 bird's eye chillies
2 saffron threads
1 bay leaf
2 thyme sprigs
salt and freshly ground black pepper

Roll the pieces of fish in the flour, making sure that they are well coated, then shake off any excess. Heat 1 tablespoon of the olive oil in a deep frying pan (skillet) and cook the fish, in batches, for 3 minutes, making sure they are lightly browned on all sides. After removing each batch from the pan, wipe it with kitchen paper (paper towels) and heat 1 tablespoon more of the olive oil before adding the next batch. Drain the cooked pieces of fish on kitchen paper (paper towels).

Using the same pan, heat 1 tablespoon olive oil and cook the shallots over a medium heat, stirring with a wooden spatula, for 3 minutes. Add the tomatoes along with the juice from the can, the tomato purée (paste) and white wine.

Tie the bird's eye chillies in a square of muslin (cheesecloth) to make them easier to remove at the end of cooking. Add the chillies, saffron threads, bay leaf and thyme and season with salt and pepper. Stir well, cover and simmer for 20 minutes over a medium heat.

Remove the lid and stir the contents of the pan. Mash the tomatoes with a fork and continue to cook over a very low heat for a further 15 minutes until thick and pulpy.

If the tomato mixture appears to be drying out during cooking, add a little more white wine, tomato juice or water. Season with salt and pepper to taste. When the sauce is almost boiling, add the monkfish pieces, stir and cook for 3 minutes over a medium heat. Check that the fish is cooked – the flesh should be white both inside and out and shouldn't break up.

Remove and discard the bird's eye chillies, bay leaf and thyme sprigs before serving with plain boiled basmati rice.

Tricks of the trade • This method enables you to prepare all the ingredients in advance. You can then reheat the sauce just before serving and finish cooking the fish as your guests sit down to eat.

Squid American Style

You can replace the monkfish (angler fish) with squid – allow about 750 g/1¾ lb for 6 servings.

Prepare the squid by pulling off the heads, removing the quill from the inside the body sacs and peeling off the fine purplish membrane from the outside – if you put salt on your hands and rub the squid, the membrane will come away easily. Cut the body sacs into rounds and cook in the same way as the monkfish (angler fish), in several batches, but you don't need to coat them in flour. Then just follow the recipe instructions given above.

Monkfish (angler fish) with green peppercorns

Serves 4
Preparation: 15 minutes
Cooking: 40 minutes

3 tablespoons green peppercorns
750 g/1½ lb monkfish (angler fish) fillet, cut into 8 pieces
about 2 tablespoons olive oil
425-g/14-oz can peeled tomatoes
50 ml/2 fl oz dry white wine
3 shallots, thinly sliced
2 tablespoons crème fraîche or natural (plain) yogurt
50 ml/2 fl oz brandy
4 tarragon sprigs, chopped
salt
To serve: sautéed potatoes

Grind up the green peppercorns fairly finely in a blender or spice grinder, tip into a bowl and mix with 1 teaspoon salt. Roll the fish pieces in the peppercorn and salt mixture, making sure they are well coated on all sides.

Heat 1 tablespoon of the olive oil in a deep frying pan (skillet) and cook the monkfish, in batches, for 3 minutes until they are lightly browned on all sides. After each batch, wipe the frying pan (skillet) with kitchen paper (paper towels) and heat 1 tablespoon more of the olive oil before adding the next batch. Place the cooked pieces of fish on kitchen paper (paper towels) between two plates to keep warm. When all the fish is cooked, add to the pan the tomatoes with the juice from the can, along the white wine and shallots, and simmer over a low heat for 30 minutes until reduced. Stir in the crème fraîche or yogurt and fish and sprinkle with brandy. Standing well back, ignite the brandy. Continue cooking for 2–3 minutes until the fish is hot. Sprinkle with chopped tarragon and serve immediately. Sautéed potatoes make an ideal accompaniment to this dish.

Tricks of the trade • You can prepare the sauce in advance, reheat it before your sit down to eat and add the fish just before serving.

Monkfish (angler fish) casserole with glazed turnips

Serves 6
Preparation: 20 minutes
Cooking: 20 minutes

1 tablespoon olive oil, plus extra for drizzling
875 g/1¾ lb turnips
1 large onion, cut into wedges
2 tablespoons clear honey
½ teaspoon ground cumin
1 kg/2 lb monkfish (angler fish) fillet
350 ml/12 fl oz/1½ cups water
sea salt and freshly ground black pepper

Heat the olive oil in a flameproof casserole and add the turnips, onion and honey. Sprinkle with cumin, season lightly with salt and pepper and mix well. Cook for 5 minutes over a fairly high heat, stirring with a wooden spatula.

Rinse the fish, pat dry with kitchen paper (paper towels) and cut into large pieces.

When the vegetables are browned, add the measured water and bring to the boil. Cover the casserole, reduce the heat to the lowest setting and cook for 10 minutes, checking occasionally that the vegetables haven't dried out, and adding a little more water if necessary.

As soon as the turnips are cooked but still slightly crisp (al dente), place the fish pieces on top of the vegetables, season with salt and pepper and drizzle with olive oil. Cover and continue cooking over a low heat for 5 minutes.

Check that the fish is cooked – it should be very white both inside and out and serve immediately.

Cod and potato casserole

Serves 6
Preparation: 15 minutes
Cooking: 25 minutes

2 tablespoons olive oil
875 g/1¾ lb waxy potatoes, scrubbed
1 large onion, cut into wedges
2 garlic cloves
2 thyme sprigs
1 bay leaf
350 ml/12 fl oz/1½ cups water
6 cod steaks, about 150 g/5 oz each
sea salt and freshly ground black pepper

Heat the olive oil in a flameproof casserole and add the potatoes, onion, garlic cloves, thyme and bay leaf. Season lightly with salt and pepper. Cook for 5 minutes over a fairly high heat, stirring with a wooden spatula. Add the measured water and bring to the boil. Cover, reduce the heat to the lowest setting and cook for 10 minutes, checking occasionally that the vegetables haven't dried out, and adding a little more water if necessary.

As soon as the potatoes are cooked but still slightly crisp (al dente), place the fish on top of the vegetables and season lightly with salt and pepper. Cover and continue cooking over a low heat for 5–7 minutes.

Check that the fish is cooked – it should have a pearly sheen both inside and out and the 'flakes' should be beginning to separate of their own accord, then serve immediately.

A few fish

Manou's bourride

Lélé's thieboudienne

Jean-Mérou's couscous

bouillabaisse

Nourithe's tagine

seafood risotto...

Coconut fish soup

Serves 6
Preparation: 25 minutes
Cooking: 30 minutes

1 kg/2 lb white fish fillets such as cod, ling, coley (pollock),
whiting or hake
2 litres/3½ pints/8¾ cups classic court-bouillon
(see page 16)
400 ml/14 fl oz 1¾ cups chicken stock
750 ml/1¼ pints/3 cups canned coconut milk
2.5-cm/1-inch of fresh root ginger, cut into thin batons
4 spring onions (scallions), thinly sliced
150 g/5 oz cellophane noodles
freshly ground black pepper
To serve: 1 bunch of coriander (cilantro), finely chopped

Rinse the fish fillets, pat dry with kitchen paper
(paper towels) and cut into pieces about 6 cm/
2½ inches long. Bring the court-bouillon to the
boil in a large pan, then lower the heat to a simmer.
Add the fish, beginning with the thickest pieces
and finishing with the thinnest. Cook for 5 minutes,
then lift out with a slotted spoon. Pat dry on kitchen paper (paper towels) and set aside.
Pour the chicken stock and coconut milk into a pan
and add the ginger and the spring onions (scallions).
Season with pepper, stir and simmer for 15 minutes.
Taste and adjust the seasoning, add the noodles
and cook for 3 minutes. Add the fish and cook for
2 minutes more.
Ladle the soup into large shallow bowls and serve
sprinkled with chopped coriander (cilantro).

Tricks of the trade • You could spice up this dish with some
sweet or hot chillies, sliced thinly and sprinkled over the soup.
If you're not a fan of cellophane noodles, serve this soup with
glutinous rice.

Fish soup

Serves 8
Preparation: 1 hour
Cooking: 1 hour 10 minutes

2 kg/2 lb Mediterranean fish, such as scorpion fish, wrasse,
sea bream (porgy), conger eel, red mullet (snapper), monkfish (angler fish), gutted, cleaned and scaled
3 tablespoons olive oil
4 leeks, white parts only sliced
4 large onions, thinly sliced
4 garlic cloves, coarsely chopped
1 bouquet garni (1 sprig each of parsley, thyme, fennel
and basil tied together)
8 tomatoes, cut into chunks
2 dried bird's eye chillies, crushed
2 pinches of saffron threads
salt and freshly ground black pepper
To serve: croûtons and rouille (see page 178)

Cut off and reserve the fish heads and tails. Cut the
fish into chunks. Cut out and discard the gills from
the fish heads.

Heat the olive oil in a large saucepan. Add the
leeks and onions and cook over a low heat, stirring
occasionally, for 15 minutes. Add the garlic and bouquet garni and cook for 5 minutes more.
Add the fish and the reserved heads, and tails.
Cook over a low heat for about 30 minutes, breaking
up the fish as the cooking progresses. Add the
tomatoes and 750 ml/1¼ pints/3 cups water, season
with salt and pepper and sprinkle with the chillies.
Bring to the boil and cook for 20 minutes.
Add the saffron. Push the soup through a food mill,
then strain it through a conical strainer to obtain
a very fine texture.
Serve immediately with croûtons and rouille.

Manou's bourride

Serves 6
Preparation: 40 minutes
Cooking: 55 minutes

200 ml/7 fl oz/scant 1 cup white wine
1 onion, chopped
3 lemon slices
thinly pared rind of 1 orange
1 thyme sprig
1 bay leaf
2 teaspoons fennel seeds
5 garlic cloves
5 egg yolks
300 ml/½ pint/1¼ cups olive oil
1.5 kg white fish, such as sea bass, hake, monkfish
(angler fish), cod, cut into chunks
2 tablespoons crème fraîche or soured (sour cream)
salt and freshly ground black pepper
To serve: steamed or boiled potatoes

Pour 1 litre/1¾ pints/4¼ cups of water into a large
pan. Add the white wine, onion, lemon slices, orange
rind, thyme, bay leaf and fennel seeds. Crush 1 garlic
clove and to the pan. Bring to the boil and simmer
for 30 minutes.
Meanwhile, prepare the aïoli (garlic mayonnaise).
Halve the remaining garlic cloves and place in a
mortar. Add 2 of the egg yolks and work the mixture
to a fine paste with a pestle. Season with salt and
pepper. Transfer the paste to a bowl and gradually
add the oil, whisking constantly until it is fully
incorporated.
Season the fish, add to the stock and simmer gently
for 15 minutes. Lift out the fish with a slotted spoon
and keep warm, covered with a ladleful of stock, on
a covered dish.
Strain the stock into a clean pan, return it to a low
heat and whisk in the aïoli. Add the remaining yolks
one at a time, whisking constantly, then stir in the
crème fraîche or cream. The sauce should be thick
and creamy. Transfer the fish to a tureen and pour
over the sauce.
Serve with steamed or boiled potatoes.

Seafood risotto

Serves 6
Preparation: 40 minutes
Cooking: 40 minutes

2 pinches of saffron threads
250 ml/8 fl oz/1 cup dry white wine
1.2 litres/2 pints/5 cups spicy or classic court-bouillon
(see page 16)
3 tablespoons olive oil
2 garlic cloves, finely chopped
1 onion, finely chopped
250 g/8 oz/1¼ cups risotto rice, preferably arborio
240-g/7½-oz can chopped tomatoes
3 tablespoons tomato purée (paste)
finely chopped rind of 1 large orange
200 g/7 oz/1¾ cups shelled peas
500 g/1 lb white fish fillets, such as cod, ling, coley (pollock), cut into chunks
18 large raw prawns (shrimp), peeled and deveined
500 g/1 lb live mussels, beards removed and scrubbed
salt and freshly ground black pepper

Dissolve the saffron in the white wine and set aside.
Pour the court-bouillon into a pan and bring to simmering point. Heat the olive oil in a large, deep
frying pan (skillet). Add the garlic and onion and
cook over a low heat, stirring occasionally, for
3–5 minutes until the onion is translucent. Add the
rice, tomatoes, tomato purée (paste), orange rind
and saffron-flavoured wine. Season with salt and
pepper and cook until all the wine is absorbed.
Add a ladleful of hot court-bouillon and cook, stirring
constantly, until it has been fully absorbed. Repeat
this process, adding the court-bouillon a ladleful at
a time and stirring constantly, until only 1 ladleful
of court-bouillon is left and the rice is creamy.
Meanwhile, cook the peas in salted, boiling water
for 7 minutes, then drain. Place the fish, prawns
(shrimp), mussels and peas on top of the rice, lower
the heat, cover and cook for 10 minutes more.
Add the last ladleful of court-bouillon.
Remove and discard any mussels that have not opened. Check that the paella is cooked through and
serve immediately.

Nourithe's tagine

Serves 6
Preparation: 10 minutes
Cooking: 30 minutes

3 tablespoons olive oil
2 tablespoons lemon juice
1 teaspoon paprika
1 teaspoon ground cumin
½ lemon, thinly sliced
1 preserved lemon, cut into small pieces
1 sweet pimiento, cut into thin strips.
2 garlic cloves, thinly sliced
2 kg/4 lb sea bream or snapper, scaled, gutted,
cleaned and thickly sliced
1 bunch fresh coriander (cilantro), coarsely chopped
salt and freshly ground black pepper
To serve: steamed potatoes

Whisk together 2 tablespoons of the olive oil, the
lemon juice, paprika, cumin and 100 ml/3½ fl oz/
scant ½ cup water in a bowl and season with salt
and pepper. Add the lemon slices, the preserved
lemon and the pimiento.
Heat the remaining olive oil in a deep frying pan
(skillet) or tagine. Add the garlic and cook over a
low heat until golden. Add the pieces of fish to the
pan, pour in the lemon mixture and sprinkle with
the coriander (cilantro). Cover and cook over a low
heat for 20 minutes. Check that the fish is cooked
through, then serve with steamed potatoes.

Bouillabaisse

Serves 6
Preparation: 30 minutes
Cooking: 45 minutes

1 teaspoon saffron threads
3 litres/5¼ pints/13 cups fish stock (see page 16)
3 tablespoons olive oil, plus extra for drizzling
5 garlic cloves, halved
4 onions, cut into small wedges
240-g/7½-oz can tomatoes
2 tablespoons tomato purée (paste)
6 waxy potatoes, chopped
1 thyme sprig
1 fennel sprig
4 flat leaf parsley sprigs
1 bay leaf
2.5 kg/5½ lb mixed fish, such as conger eel, scorpion fish,
sea bream (porgy), sea bass, red mullet or snapper, scaled,
gutted and cleaned
salt and freshly ground black pepper
To serve: croûtons, freshly grated Parmesan cheese and
rouille (see page 178)

Put the saffron in a small bowl and stir in 175 ml/
6 fl oz/¾ cup of the fish stock and set aside. Heat
the olive oil in a large pan. Add the garlic and onions
and cook over a very low heat, stirring occasionally,
for 30 minutes.
Meanwhile, pour the remaining fish stock into another pan and bring to the boil. Lower the heat to a
simmer and add the tomatoes, tomato purée
(paste), potatoes, thyme, fennel, parsley, bay leaf
and saffron-flavoured stock.
Cut any large fish into chunks. Add the fish to the
pan of onions in the following order: firm-fleshed
fish such as conger eel, then the scorpion fish, sea
bream (porgy) and sea bass and, finally, the red mullet or snapper. Season with salt and pepper, drizzle
in some olive oil and pour in the boiling fish stock.
Cook over a high heat for 12 minutes.
Lift out the fish and arrange in a warm, deep serving dish. Remove and discard the herbs and ladle
the soup over the fish. Serve immediately
with croûtons, grated cheese, and rouille.

Variation • If you feel up to the effort, you could make this
dish even more delicious by replacing the fish stock with
homemade fish soup (see page 98). You can also buy very good
fish soup in cartons.

Couscous 'Francius', a.k.a. Jean-Mérou's couscous

Serves 8
Preparation: 1 hour
Cooking: 1 hour 10 minutes
Marinating: 24 hours

FOR THE FISH STOCK:
**fish heads and trimmings, including a grouper steak
and head if possible**
2 onions
1 clove
3 garlic cloves, crushed
2 bay leaves
2 thyme sprigs
3 tablespoons olive oil
1 tablespoon coarse sea salt
1 tablespoon black peppercorns

FOR THE COUSCOUS:
**2.5 kg/5½ lb mixed fish fillets, such as scorpion fish,
sea bream (porgy), grouper, pandora or sea bass, grey mullet or snapper**
4 tablespoons coarse sea salt
4 teaspoons ground cumin
4 tablespoons olive oil
4 large onions, cut into wedges
2 small cans tomato purée (paste), about 140 g/4½ oz each
3 tablespoons ras-el-hanout spice mixture (see below)
3 courgettes (zucchini)
1 green chilli
1 teaspoon black peppercorns
8 carrots, halved
4 medium turnips
2 fennel bulbs, halved
½ green cabbage, cut into 4 pieces
240-g/7½-oz can chickpeas (garbanzos)
750 g/1½ lb/4 cups very fine couscous
25 g/1 oz/2 tablespoons butter, cut into small pieces
salt

Ras-el-hanout • 1 tablespoon ground coriander seeds •
1 tablespoon ground cumin • 1 tablespoon ground ginger •
1 tablespoon ground pepper • ½ teaspoon ground mace •
½ teaspoon ground nutmeg • ½ teaspoon allspice •
½ teaspoon ground cardamon • ½ teaspoon turmeric •
½ teaspoon ground cinnamon • ¼ teaspoon ground cloves
• ¼ teaspoon cayenne pepper

Combine all ingredients and store in a container with a
tightly-fitting lid.

Start by preparing the fish for the couscous. Rinse
the fish fillets and pat dry with kitchen paper (paper
towels). Mix together the sea salt and ground cumin
on a large shallow plate. Coat the fish in the mixture, place on a large plate and cover with clingfilm
(plastic wrap). Leave in the refrigerator
for 24 hours to marinate.

For the fish stock, cut out and discard the gills from
the fish heads. Spike one of the onions with the
clove. Place the heads, trimmings, grouper steak,
if using, garlic, onions, bay leaves, thyme, olive oil,
coarse salt and peppercorns in a stock pot or large
flameproof casserole. Cover with 3 litres/5¼ pints/
13 cups water, bring to the boil, then lower the heat
and simmer for 15 minutes. Strain the stock into a
bowl. Skin the pieces of fish and remove the bones.
Add the flesh to the stock and keep warm.

Heat the olive oil in a large pan. Add the onions and
cook over a medium heat, stirring occasionally, for
5 minutes until golden. Lower the heat and add the
tomato purée (paste) and the ras-el-hanout and
pour in 250 ml/8 fl oz/1 cup of the fish stock. Stir
well, cover and cook for 15 minutes.

Meanwhile, slice the courgettes in half widthways,
then again in half lengthways. Remove the fish fillets
from the refrigerator and rinse under cold running
water. Add the whole of the remaining fish stock to
the pan along with the chilli and peppercorns. Stir
well and season to taste with salt.

Add the carrots, cover and simmer gently for
10 minutes. Add the turnips and fennel, re-cover
the pan and simmer for a further 10 minutes.
Finally, add the cabbage, courgettes (zucchini),
chickpeas (garbanzos) and the fish. Cover and cook
for a further 12 minutes.

Meanwhile, prepare the couscous according to the
instructions on the packet. When it's ready, stir in
the pieces of butter.

Remove and discard the chilli from the fish mixture.
Serve the couscous, vegetables and fish on warm
plates, with plenty of stock ladled over them.

Tricks of the trade • The ultimate way to make this couscous
is to use grouper only, but it's an expensive fish and may not
be available. You may be able to order it in advance, in which
case, specify that you'll need the head to make the fish stock.
Always choose your fish by its freshness. If you can't get hold
of grouper, never mind – choose one or more varieties of white
(non-oily) fish that fire your enthusiasm.

Lélé's thieboudienne (Senegalese fish and rice stew)

Serves 8
1 hour preparation time
1 hour cooking time

2.5 kg/5½ lb mixed fish, such as scorpion fish, sea bream (porgy), sea bass, hake, scaled if necessary, gutted, cleaned and cut into large chunks
½ bunch of flat leaf parsley, leaves only
2 garlic cloves, halved
4 small dried bird's eye chillies
6 tablespoons olive oil
4 onions, cut into wedges
50 g/2 oz yète, well-rinsed (optional)
300 g/10 oz tomato purée (paste)
400-g/13-oz can tomatoes
1 fresh habanero chilli
2 stock (bouillon) cubes ('jumbo' cubes if available)
1 aubergine (eggplant), cut into 1-cm/½-inch slices
2 courgettes (zucchini)
4 carrots, halved
100 g/3½ oz dried fish (guedj if available; optional)
8 small turnips
½ firm, round cabbage, cut into 4 pieces
salt and freshly ground black pepper
To serve: 625 g/1¼ lb rice ('broken rice' if available) cooked

Rinse the fresh fish well and pat dry on kitchen paper (paper towels).

To prepare the stuffing, put the parsley leaves, garlic and dried chillies in a blender, season with pepper and process to combine.

Prick the pieces of fish with a fork and then stuff them with the mixture. Place them on a plate, cover with clingfilm (plastic wrap) and chill in the refrigerator until required.

Heat half the olive oil in a large pan. Add the onions and yète, if using, and cook over a medium heat, stirring occasionally, for 5 minutes until the onions are golden. Add the tomato purée (tomato paste), tomatoes, habanero chilli, stock (bouillon) cubes and 2 litres/3½ pints/8¾ cups water. Bring to the boil. Meanwhile, halve the aubergine (eggplant) slices and slice the courgettes (zucchini) in half widthways, then again in half lengthways.

Season the stock to taste with salt and add the carrots and the guedj. Lower the heat, cover and simmer gently for 10 minutes. Add the turnips and aubergine (eggplant), re-cover the pan and cook for a further 10 minutes.

Meanwhile, heat the remaining olive oil in a large frying pan (skillet). Add the pieces of fish and cook, turning occasionally, until lightly browned. Remove from the pan and drain on kitchen paper (paper towels). Add the cabbage, courgettes (zucchini) and fish to the pan of vegetables, re-cover and cook for 12 minutes.

Lift out the vegetables and fish, and place on two separate plates. Remove and discard the yète and the guedj. Serve with the broken rice.

Tricks of the trade • You'll find yète (a large dried mollusc), guedj (dried fish), 'jumbo' stock cubes and broken rice in African grocery stores.

Raw fish

or how to become a Sushi Master

Kenji Imamura, Sushi Master

The art of preparing raw fish

There are three main ways of preparing raw fish: tartare, carpaccio and sushi or sashimi. The most important thing is for the fish to be really fresh. Don't store the raw ingredients for long, and consume the finished dish without delay. Good, well-sharpened knives are absolutely essential.

Carpaccio of fish

How can you cut those paper-thin slices if the flesh of the fish is soft? The secret is to put the fish in the freezer for 1 hour to firm it up, before slicing it thinly with a very well-sharpened knife. Arrange the slices on plates brushed with olive oil, which can be left in the refrigerator for a few minutes, covered with clingfilm (plastic wrap). Season the fish just before serving.

The process is the same when starting off with fish fillets. If you are dealing with steaks, slicing will be easier, since the fish is of the same thickness throughout.

Fish tartare

Equip yourself with two very good knives. First cut the fish fillet or steak into large chunks, then chop each chunk by crossing the two knives. Whatever you do, don't chop the fish in a food processor, or you'll end up with a purée. You can season the tartare generously before serving it, and leave it in the refrigerator. On the other hand, if you are adding lemon juice, stir it in only at the very last minute or it will 'cook' the flesh of the fish.

Sushi and sashimi

Use a very well sharpened knife to prepare the small fish fillets that will be used in your sushi or that you will eat as sashimi. Cut the fish fillets from top to bottom into 6-cm/2½-inch wide strips, then slice each strip against the grain of the fish into 5-mm/¼-inch wide slices.

Smoked fish and apple tartare

Serves 4
Preparation: 15 minutes

1 tart eating apple
125 ml/4 fl oz/½ cup lemon juice
400 g/13 oz very fresh smoked haddock or smoked cod, skinned and cut into chunks
4 tablespoons olive oil
½ red onion, finely diced
½ bunch of chives, finely chopped
freshly ground black pepper

Peel and core the apple, then dice finely and sprinkle with half the lemon juice to prevent it
from turning brown.
Coarsely chop the chunks of fish using 2 very sharp knives. Prepare a dressing by whisking together the remaining lemon juice and the olive oil in a bowl. Season with pepper.
Add the apple, onion and fish to the bowl and toss gently. Divide among 4 plates and sprinkle with the chives. Don't add any extra salt – the fish is already salty enough.

Tuna and pine nut tartare

Serves 4
Preparation: 15 minutes

2 tablespoons pine nuts
2 handfuls of rocket (arugula)
½ bunch of chervil
3 tablespoons hazelnut oil
dash of Tabasco sauce
400 g/13 oz very fresh tuna fillet, cut into chunks
sea salt and freshly ground black pepper
To serve: Parmesan cheese shavings

Dry-fry the pine nuts in a very hot pan for about
a minute.
Put the pine nuts, rocket (arugula), chervil, hazelnut oil and Tabasco in a food processor and season with salt and pepper. Pulse briefly, taking care not to reduce the mixture to a purée. Transfer to a bowl.
Coarsely chop the chunks of tuna using 2 well-sharpened knives. Add the fish to the bowl and
toss gently with the dressing.
Divide among serving plates, sprinkle with sea salt and season with a little pepper. Serve garnished with a few Parmesan shavings.

Cod tartare with herbs

Serves 4
Preparation: 15 minutes

400 g/13 oz very fresh cod fillet, skinned and cut into chunks
8 chive stalks, coarsely chopped
4 coriander (cilantro) sprigs, coarsely chopped
4 chervil sprigs, coarsely chopped
2 flat leaf parsley sprigs, coarsely chopped
2 tarragon sprigs, coarsely chopped
2 spring onions (scallions), white parts chopped and green parts sliced
2 tablespoons olive oil
2 tablespoons hazelnut oil
sea salt and freshly ground black pepper
To serve: green salad (salad greens) and toasted rustic bread

Chop the cod with 2 very sharp knives and place on a large plate. Add all the herbs and the spring onions (scallions) and mix gently. Drizzle over both types of oil and season with sea salt and pepper. Serve well chilled, accompanied by a green salad (salad greens) and toasted rustic bread.

Variation • You can further enhance the flavour of this tartare by grinding up a few fresh hazelnuts and sprinkling them over the fish.

Raw marinated sardines

Serves 6–8
Preparation: 20 minutes
Marinating: 1 hour

20 very fresh sardines, scaled, gutted, cleaned and filleted
100 ml/3½ fl oz/scant ½ cup olive oil
150 ml/¼ pint/⅔ cup lime juice
10 coriander (cilantro) sprigs, finely chopped
4 spring onions (scallions), white parts chopped and
green parts sliced
4 tablespoons pine nuts
1 baguette or rustic loaf, sliced
2–3 tablespoons crème fraîche or soured (sour) cream
salt and freshly ground black pepper

Rinse the sardines and pat dry with kitchen paper (paper towels). Mix together the olive oil, lime juice, chopped coriander (cilantro), and the white and green parts of the spring onions (scallions) in a bowl. Season with salt and pepper.

Arrange one-third of the sardines in a non-metallic dish and pour one-third of the marinade over them. Continue layering the sardines, finishing with the marinade. Sprinkle with the pine nuts. Cover the dish with clingfilm (plastic wrap) and chill in the refrigerator for at least 1 hour.

Just before serving, toast the slices of bread on both sides and spread them with a little crème fraîche or cream. Season lightly with pepper, top with the marinated sardines and drizzle with a little of the marinade. You can also eat these without the bread and with or without crème fraîche, according to taste.

Spinach and tuna

Serves 4
Preparation: 20 minutes

300 g/10 oz very fresh tuna fillet
4 tablespoons olive oil
1/2 teaspoon wasabi paste
2 handfuls of baby spinach leaves
8 sun-dried tomatoes in oil, drained and thinly sliced
1/2 bunch of coriander (cilantro), finely chopped
1 tablespoon soy sauce
sea salt and freshly ground black pepper

Rinse the tuna, pat dry with kitchen paper (paper towels) and cut it into small cubes.
Whisk together the olive oil and wasabi paste in a salad bowl. Add the soy sauce and season to taste with pepper.
Just before serving, toss the spinach in the dressing with the tuna and sun-dried tomatoes and sprinkle with the coriander (cilantro). Taste and adjust the seasoning, bearing in mind that the soy sauce is already quite salty.

Variation • You could also add a few pine nuts to this salad for a contrasting crunch, as well as some lightly toasted sesame seeds.

Tuna with sesame sauce

Serves 4
Preparation: 20 minutes
Cooking: 5 minutes

625 g/1 1/4 lb very fresh tuna fillet
100 g/3 1/2 oz/scant 1/2 cup sesame seeds
2 teaspoons sesame oil
1 tablespoon soy sauce
2 tablespoons mirin
3 teaspoons caster (superfine) sugar
75 g/3 oz instant dashi granules
250 ml/8 fl oz/1 cup hot water

Rinse the tuna, pat dry with kitchen paper (paper towels) and cut into 6-cm/2 1/2-inch wide strips. Slice each strip against the grain into 5-mm/1/4-inch thick slices. Place these slices around the edge of a round plate, leaving enough room in the middle for a bowl of dipping sauce. Cover the plate with cling-film (plastic wrap) and chill in the refrigerator until ready to serve.
Dry-fry the sesame seeds in a hot pan, stirring constantly, for 3–5 minutes until golden. Crush the seeds in a mortar with a pestle, add the sesame oil and stir to form a paste. Mix this paste with the soy sauce, mirin, sugar, dashi granules and hot water. Leave to cool. Serve the tuna well chilled with the cold dipping sauce.

Tricks of the trade • You can keep the sauce for 2 days in a cool place. You'll find the mirin (sweet rice wine) and dashi (dehydrated fish stock) in some supermarkets and Japanese food stores.

Salmon sashimi

Serves 6–8
Preparation: 20 minutes

625 g/1 1/4 lb very fresh salmon fillets, skinned
1 teaspoon wasabi paste
125 ml/4 fl oz/1/2 cup soy sauce

Rinse the fish, pat dry with kitchen paper (paper towels) and remove any remaining pin bones with tweezers. Cut the salmon into 6-cm/2 1/2-inch wide strips and slice each strip against the grain into 5-mm/1/4-inch thick slices.
For the dipping sauce, mix together the wasabi paste and soy sauce in a small bowl. (You can add more wasabi if you like.) Place the fish on a plate and serve with the bowl of dipping sauce in the centre.

Tricks of the trade • You can prepare the fish in advance and store, covered with clingfilm (plastic wrap), in the refrigerator (plastic wrap) until ready to serve. Do not put the dipping sauce in the refrigerator. You can also make this recipe with tuna, sea bream (porgy), sea bass or perch.

Sea bream (porgy) carpaccio with lime

Serves 4
Preparation: 30 minutes
Freezing: 1 hour

4 very fresh sea bream (porgy) fillets,
75-100 g/3–3½ oz each, skinned
3 tablespoons olive oil
1½ tablespoons lime juice
a few chive sprigs, finely chopped
sea salt and freshly ground black pepper

Rinse the fish fillets and pat dry with kitchen paper (paper towels). Wrap them in clingfilm (plastic wrap) and place in the freezer for about 1 hour. While the fish is chilling, brush 4 plates with a little of the olive oil. Whisk the remaining olive oil with the lime juice to make a dressing.
As soon as the fillets are firm enough to slice, use a long, flexible, well-sharpened knife to carve through the thickness of the fish at an angle, starting from the centre of the fillet. Arrange the slices and any small leftover pieces on the plates. Cover each plate with clingfilm (plastic wrap) and chill in the refrigerator until ready to serve.
Just before serving, drizzle each plate with the dressing and sprinkle with salt and pepper and some chopped chives.

Trout preserved in oil

Serves 6–8
Preparation: 25 minutes
Marinating: 12 hours

625 g/1¼ lb very fresh trout fillets
2 white onions, thinly sliced into rings
250 ml/8 fl oz/1 cup sunflower oil
rustic bread
6–8 tablespoons crème fraîche or soured (sour) cream
sea salt and freshly ground black pepper

Wash the fish fillets, pat dry with kitchen paper (paper towels) and remove any remaining pin bones with tweezers. Using a well-sharpened knife, cut the fillets into 1-cm/½-inch thick slices.
Place a few slices of trout in a sterilised glass preserving jar, then add a few onion rings. Make alternating layers until all the ingredients are used up. Pour the oil into the jar and seal tightly. Leave to marinate in the refrigerator for 12 hours.
Just before serving, toast some slices of rustic bread and serve the fish on the toast with a few onion rings from the marinade and a spoonful of crème fraîche or cream. Season with salt and pepper.

Thai-style carpaccio

Serves 4
Preparation: 30 minutes
Freezing: 1 hour
Marinating: 1½ hours

400 g/13 oz very fresh swordfish fillet
grated rind and juice of ½ lime
3 tablespoons sesame oil
1 lemon grass stalk, thinly sliced
1 tablespoon sesame seeds
sea salt and freshly ground black pepper

Rinse the fish and pat dry with kitchen paper. Wrap it in clingfilm (plastic wrap) and place in the freezer for about 1 hour.
Meanwhile, mix together the lime rind and juice, sesame oil and lemon grass in a bowl and season with salt and pepper. Set aside in a cool place.
As soon as the fillet is fairly firm, cut into very thin slices with a long, well-sharpened knife. Arrange the slices on 4 plates and strain a little of the lime marinade over each. Cover each plate with clingfilm (plastic wrap) and leave in a cool place for 30 minutes to marinate.
Dry-fry the sesame seeds in a hot pan for 3–5 minutes until golden brown. Just before serving, sprinkle the fish with the sesame seeds and season with salt and pepper.

Sea bream (porgy) tartare

Serves 4
Preparation: 30 minutes
Cooking: 30 minutes

300 g/10 oz/1¼ cups Puy lentils
5 tablespoons olive oil
400 g/13 oz very fresh sea bream (porgy) fillets, skinned
and cut into chunks
3 tablespoons lime juice
½ bunch of fresh coriander (cilantro), chopped
4-cm/1¾-inch piece of fresh root ginger, sliced into
thin batons
sea salt and freshly ground black pepper

Put the lentils in a large pan and cover with water. Bring to the boil, then simmer for 30–45 minutes until tender but not mushy. Heat 1 tablespoon of the olive oil in a small pan and sauté the ginger for 5 minutes. Drain on kitchen paper (paper towels) and leave to cool.
Using 2 knives, coarsely chop the fish.
Mix together the lime juice and remaining olive oil in a bowl and season with salt and pepper. Place the lentils, ginger, fish and coriander (cilantro) in a serving bowl and mix together gently. Pour over the dressing and toss lightly.
Serve chilled, sprinkled with salt and pepper.

Sushi

Serves 6–8
Preparation: 40 minutes
Resting: 30 minutes
Cooking: 30 minutes

450 g/14½ oz/generous 2 cups Japanese rice
1 tablespoon caster (superfine) sugar
1 teaspoon salt
200 ml/7 fl oz/scant 1 cup rice vinegar
400 g/13 oz very fresh fish fillets, such as sea bream
(porgy), salmon or tuna
1–2 teaspoons wasabi paste
To serve: soy sauce, for dipping

Wash the rice is several changes of water until the water runs clear, then drain and leave to rest for 30 minutes.

Place the rice in a pan and pour in 600 ml/1 pint/ 2½ cups water. Cover and bring to the boil over a high heat. Lower the heat to medium and cook for 10 minutes, then reduce the heat again and cook for a further 5 minutes. Remove the pan from the heat and set aside, still covered, for 10–15 minutes. Meanwhile, put the sugar, salt and rice vinegar in a small pan and heat until the sugar and salt dissolve. When the grains have swollen, tip the rice into a bowl and drizzle over the vinegar mixture, stirring gently with a wooden spatula. Set aside to cool, but don't put it in the refrigerator.

Cut the fish fillets into 6-cm/2½-inch wide strips, then slice each strip against the grain into 5-mm/ ¼-inch thick slices.

As soon as the rice is completely cold, wring out a wet tea towel (dish towel) that you can use to keep your hands moist. Shape the rice into small, squat sausage shapes with the hollow of your hand.

Spread a little wasabi paste on each portion of rice and place a piece of fish on top.

Serve immediately with soy sauce for dipping – sushi doesn't take well to chilling.

At low tide...

Breton lobster

mussels

langoustines

prawns (shrimp)

green shore crab

Bivalves

Cockles

Cockles may be eaten raw or cooked, but most people prefer them cooked. First make sure that they're alive and discard any that are already open. Soak them in cold, salted water for at least 1 hour to get rid of any sand. Stir the water well, then leave them to soak before lifting them out carefully to avoid disturbing the sand settled on the bottom of the container. Sauté the cockles in a pan for 3-4 minutes, until they open. If you are using the cooking juices, strain them through a conical strainer or fine muslin (cheesecloth).

Queen scallops

Insist on your supplier providing you with fresh queen scallops, still in their shells. They are best served cooked – sautéed, baked, steamed, or poached in court-bouillon. Clean them thoroughly and place under the grill (broiler); once they are all open, drizzle them with some olive oil and lemon juice and enjoy them piping hot. They are known familiarly as queenies.

Littleneck clams

Littleneck clams can be brown, white, yellow and patterned. These are also known as hard-shell or quahog clams. They may be eaten raw or cooked, but must first be opened. One way to do this is to slip the tip of a knife into the black muscle at the side. Before preparing them, make sure that they're all alive: they should be tightly closed. Leave them in cold, salted water for several hours to get rid of any sand, then heat them in a large pan until they all open. Discard any that do not open.

Warty venus clams

Choose the largest ones if you can – they are the best. They may be eaten raw or cooked. To wash and open them, proceed as for the littlenecks. They are equally good steamed over a spicy stock for 10 minutes, braised or baked in a gratin for 5-6 minutes. They are also known as prairies.

Dog cockles

These small bivalves, which are not actually cockles, have distinctive brownish zigzag patterns on their shells. They are found around the coasts of Europe but are only really eaten on the continent (in France they are known as amandes). If you do manage to get hold of some, treat them like cockles. Always check for freshness: a gaping bivalve should close immediately when the shell is tapped. Wash in plenty of water and discard any that are partially open and don't close when tapped, then drain on a tea towel (dish towel). Dog cockles may be eaten raw or cooked. To cook, sauté them in a large pan until they are all open, then add a sauce or topping and bake in a preheated oven, 240°C (475°F), gas mark 9, for 3-4 minutes. Or try cooking them with pastis (see recipe p. 130).

Stuffed littleneck clams

Serves 6
Preparation: 15 minutes
Cooking: 8-10 minutes

36 littleneck clams
65 g/2½ oz/5 tablespoons butter, softened
1 shallot, chopped
2 parsley sprigs, chopped
pinch of freshly grated nutmeg
6 tablespoons fine fresh breadcrumbs
white pepper

Wash the clams in plenty of salted water, then spread them out them on a baking sheet and place in a preheated oven, 220°C (425°F), gas mark 7, for about 5 minutes, until they have opened. Discard any clams that do not open.
Remove from the oven and drain the juices into a bowl. Add the butter and beat to combine, then beat in the shallot, parsley and nutmeg and season with white pepper. Top the clams with this mixture, sprinkle with breadcrumbs and cook under a preheated grill (broiler) for 3-5 minutes, about 10 cm/4 inches from the heat. Make sure they cook very gently.
Serve as soon as the topping is golden brown, but watch your fingers – the clams will be very hot.

Cockles with pastis

Serves 6
Preparation: 5 minutes
Cooking: 10 minutes

3 litres/5¼ pints/13 cups cockles (about 72 in total)
3 star anise
2 tablespoons pastis
sea salt and freshly ground black pepper
To serve: buttered toasted rustic bread

Wash the cockles as described on page 128. Place them in a large pan with the star anise. Mix the pastis with 100 ml/3½ fl oz/scant ½ cup water and add to the pan.
Cover the pan (preferably with a glass lid, so you can keep an eye on the cockles as they cook) and set over a medium heat. As soon as you hear a little whistle, lower the heat and continue cooking for 8 minutes, shaking the pan frequently so that all the cockles remain in contact with the heat. Do not uncover the pan as you want to keep all the steam inside. As soon as the cockles are ready, serve them with buttered toasted rustic bread.

Cockles with coriander (cilantro)

Serves 4
Preparation: 15 minutes
Cooking: 10 minutes

2 litres/3½ pints/8¾ cups cockles
1 tablespoon olive oil
2 shallots, coarsely chopped
175 ml/6 fl oz/¾ cup dry white wine
50 ml/2 fl oz/¼ cup crème fraîche or soured (sour) cream
½ bunch of coriander (cilantro), finely chopped
freshly ground black pepper

Wash the cockles as described on page 128. Heat the olive oil in a deep frying pan (skillet). Add the shallots, cover and cook over a low heat for 2-3 minutes. Add the cockles and white wine and season with pepper. Increase the heat to high, cover and cook, shaking the pan occasionally, for 3-5 minutes until they open. Discard any cockles that do not open.
Remove the pan from the heat and strain the cockles, reserving the cooking liquid. Return the cockles to the pan to keep warm.
Strain the cooking liquid through a strainer lined with muslin (cheesecloth) into a saucepan. Stir in the cream and cook for 3 minutes over a medium heat, without letting it boil. Pour the sauce over the cockles and stir in the coriander (cilantro). Serve immediately as a very laid-back appetizer, since your friends are bound to get the delicious juices all over their hands – don't forget the napkins or the finger bowls.

Baked queen scallops

Serves 6
Preparation: 10 minutes
Cooking: 5-10 minutes

72 queen scallops in their shells
15 g/½ oz/1 tablespoon butter
1 tablespoon olive oil
1 tablespoon lemon juice
freshly ground black pepper

Line the grill (broiler) pan with foil and place the scallops on it. Place under a preheated grill (broiler) for 5–10 minutes until they open. Discard any scallops that do not open. Remove the jagged skirt and black gut.
Meanwhile, melt the butter with the olive oil, lemon juice and a little pepper. As soon as the scallops have opened, drizzle them with the melted butter and enjoy them without delay.

Linguini with shellfish and bacon

Serves 6
Preparation: 50 minutes
Cooking: 15 minutes

1 litre/1³/₄ pints/scant 4¹/₂ cups large cockles
500 g/1 lb warty venus clams
500 g/1 lb littleneck clams
15 g/¹/₂ oz/1 tablespoon butter
2 shallots
2 thyme sprigs
350 ml/12 fl oz/1¹/₂ cups dry white wine
200 ml/7 fl oz/scant 1 cup double (heavy) cream
150 g/5 oz smoked bacon, diced
500 g/1 lb linguini
100 g/3¹/₂ oz Parmesan cheese, shaved
¹/₂ bunch of chives, chopped
salt and freshly ground black pepper

Wash the shellfish as described on page 128. Melt the butter in a large pan. Add the shallots, cover and cook over a low heat for 2–3 minutes. Add the shellfish, thyme and wine and season with pepper. Increase the heat to high, cover and cook, shaking the pan occasionally, for 3-5 minutes until all the shells have opened. Discard any shells that do not open.

Remove the pan from the heat and strain the shellfish, reserving the cooking liquid. Then strain the cooking liquid though a strainer lined with a piece of muslin (cheesecloth) into a large, deep frying pan (skillet) or wok. Stir in the cream and set over a very low heat.

In another pan cook the diced bacon over a high heat for 3 minutes. Bring a large pan of salted water to the boil. Meanwhile, remove the cockles and clams from their shells and set aside.

Cook the pasta in the pan of boiling, salted water for 2 minutes less than specified on the instructions on the packet: it should be slightly underdone.

Add 2 ladlefuls of the pasta cooking water to the cream mixture. Drain the pasta.

Tip the bacon and shellfish into the frying pan (skillet) or wok, then add the pasta. Stir to combine and continue cooking for 2-3 minutes until the pasta is al dente.

Serve immediately in deep plates, seasoned with pepper and sprinkled with Parmesan shavings and chopped chives.

Tricks of the trade • If the warty venus and littleneck clams are bigger than the cockles, cook the shellfish separately — the cockles on their own and the clams together. You could also make this dish with just cockles, if you prefer, in which case you'll need 2 litres/3¹/₂ pints/8³/₄ cups.
This recipe may be made ahead of time. Prepare all the ingredients and reheat the sauce very gently at the last minute, then cook the linguini and proceed as described above.

Gastropods

Winkles

The operculum, which covers the opening to the shell, should be firmly attached and the winkles should exude a smell of the sea. Discard any where the operculum is not tightly shut. Rinse well, place in a saucepan filled with cold water and bring to the boil. Cook for 3 minutes.

Whelks

Whelks don't respond well to refrigeration, so make sure they don't smell unpleasant when you buy them. Rinse in warm water, scrub with a brush and soak them in several changes of salted water, finishing with fresh water – a total of three 1-hour soaks. To cook, place them in a pan with cold water to cover, bring to the boil, lower the heat and simmer gently for 5 minutes.

Whelks with star anise

Serves 4
Preparation: 5 minutes
Cooking: 5 minutes

1.5 kg/3 lb whelks
2 tablespoons coarse sea salt
1 thyme sprig
1 bay leaf
1 teaspoon black peppercorns
6 star anise

Wash the whelks thoroughly and place them in a large pan of cold water. Add the salt, thyme, bay leaf, peppercorns and star anise. Bring to the boil, then lower the heat and simmer for 5 minutes. Tip the whelks into a strainer and allow them to cool before serving.

Variation • The star anise can be replaced by 2 teaspoons chilli powder, in which case don't add the peppercorns.
You might wish to pass round a good home-made Mayonnaise (see page 178) with the whelks, unless you're worried that this might overpower their hint of star anise.

Large bivalve shellfish

Scallops

Scallops are eaten raw or cooked. Make sure they're alive when you buy them – they should close at once when the white flesh is gently touched.

To open the scallops, holding the shell flat side uppermost, insert a fairly broad knife just in front of the hinge, keeping the blade against the shell. Feel for the muscle holding the two shells together and sever it. Open the scallop, rinse under cold running water, remove the jagged skirt and the black gut, then slide the blade of the knife under the white muscle, as close as possible to the shell, and detach it. Rinse in cold water.

The classic cooking method is to sauté them for 1 minute on each side, then seasoning them.

The French call scallops 'coquilles St Jacques' – St James's shells. Pilgrims on their way to visit the saint's tomb at Santiago di Compostella wear scallop-shaped badges as they proceed along the famous trail.

Sautéed scallops with garlic and pastis

Serves 4
Preparation: 20 minutes
Cooking: 2 minutes

16 scallops, shelled
2 tablespoons olive oil
2 garlic cloves, finely chopped
2 tablespoons pastis
sea salt and freshly ground black pepper
To serve: green salad (salad greens), olive oil

Rinse the scallops under cold running water and pat dry with kitchen paper (paper towels). Heat the olive oil in a large sauté pan or frying pan (skillet). Add the scallops and garlic and cook over a high heat for 1 minute on each side. Add the pastis and ignite. When the flames have died down, season with sea salt and pepper.
Serve immediately with a green salad (salad greens) dressed with olive oil.

Tricks of the trade • If you don't have a large deep frying pan (skillet), cook the scallops in two batches. Keep the first batch hot between 2 plates and wipe your pan clean with kitchen paper (paper towels), then heat a little more olive oil and sauté the second batch. You could also replace the garlic with 16 basil leaves, in which case season the scallops generously with pepper, but don't flambé them with the pastis. Simple and delicious!

Scallop broth

Serves 4
Preparation: 20 minutes
Cooking: 35 minutes
Marinating: 30 minutes minimum

16 scallops, shelled
3 tablespoons lime juice
1 tablespoon olive oil
3 lemon grass stalks, cut into short lengths
1.5-cm/3/4-inch piece of fresh root ginger, grated
4 carrots, sliced
1 leek, sliced lengthways and cut into short lengths
1 onion, cut into thin wedges
1/2 bunch of coriander (cilantro), finely chopped
salt and freshly ground black pepper

Discard the corals or reserve for another recipe. Rinse the scallops under cold running water and pat dry with kitchen paper (paper towels). Place on a plate and sprinkle with half the lime juice and the olive oil and season with salt and pepper. Cover with clingfilm (plastic wrap) and set aside in a cool place for 1 hour.
Bring 1 litre/13/4 pints/41/4 cups water to the boil. Add the lemon grass and ginger and season with salt and pepper. Simmer for 20 minutes. Strain the broth and return it to the pan. Add the carrots, leek and onion and simmer gently for 10 minutes. Add the remaining lime juice, then taste and adjust the seasoning if necessary.

Ladle the broth into soup plates and divide the scallops between them. Sprinkle with the coriander (cilantro) and leave to stand for 5 minutes until the scallops are al dente, then serve.

Tricks of the trade • The scallops should marinate for a minimum of 30 minutes but can be left somewhere cool or in the refrigerator for longer than this if necessary. You can prepare this recipe in two stages, cook the vegetables, reheat the broth at the last moment, then add the scallops to finish it off. That way you won't be stuck in the kitchen while your guests are having their aperitif or appetizer.

Scallops with a creamy coral sauce

Serves 4
Preparation: 20 minutes
Cooking: 15 minutes

16 scallops, shelled and including corals
1 shallot, coarsely chopped
2 tablespoons white wine vinegar
2 tarragon sprigs, leaves only
1 garlic clove, finely chopped
15 g/1/2 oz/1 tablespoon butter
2 tablespoons crème fraîche or soured (sour) cream
1 tablespoon olive oil
sea salt and freshly ground black pepper
To serve: braised leeks (see page 184)

Rinse the scallops under cold running water and pat them dry with kitchen paper (paper towels). Separate the corals from the white muscle. Place the shallot, vinegar, tarragon leaves and garlic in a small pan over a medium heat and cook until reduced. Then add the butter and season with salt and pepper. Remove from the heat. Quickly sauté the corals on all sides in a nonstick frying pan (skillet) – this should take less than 1 minute. Place the corals, crème fraîche or cream and the shallot mixture in a blender or food processor and pulse several times until smooth. Strain the sauce through a very fine strainer into a bowl.
Season the scallops with salt and pepper. Heat the olive oil in a large, deep frying pan (skillet). Add the scallops and cook over a high heat for 1 minute on each side. Remove from the heat, stir in the coral cream and serve immediately with braised leeks.

Scallop carpaccio with truffle oil

Serves 4
Preparation: 30 minutes
Freezing: 1 hour

8 scallops, shelled
truffle oil, for brushing and drizzling
sea salt and freshly ground black pepper

Rinse the scallops under cold running water and pat dry with kitchen paper (paper towels). Wrap them in clingfilm (plastic wrap) and place in the freezer for 1 hour.

Meanwhile, prepare the plates by brushing them with the truffle oil.

As soon as the scallops are fairly firm, remove them from the freezer and slice into 3-mm/⅛-inch thick slices with a well-sharpened knife. Arrange them in a rosette on each plate. Cover the plates with clingfilm (plastic film) and leave in a cool place until ready to serve.

Just before serving, drizzle the scallops with truffle oil and season with sea salt and pepper.

Tricks of the trade • Don't overdo the truffle oil as it has a very strong flavour: 1 teaspoon per plate is plenty. You could replace the truffle oil with a little extra virgin olive oil mixed with a few drops of lemon juice and add some toasted pine nuts. You could also underscore the truffle flavour by sprinkling the scallops with thin slices of truffle, shaved at the last minute. You'll find truffle oil in good delicatessens.

Pearl shellfish

Oysters

Oysters are eaten raw or cooked. There are numerous varieties, distinguished by their size, taste and texture. The European fines de claires no. 2 are recommended for their slight hazelnut taste. Other important varieties are native British, Pacific, Virginian, Cape and Chesapeake Bay oysters.

Always buy live oysters that give off a pleasant, fresh shellfish smell. They don't stand up at all well to refrigeration, but if you open them all before eating them, they must be kept cool and consumed within 18 hours. If you're not opening them immediately, store in a basket in a cool, dark place for up to 4–5 days.

An oyster knife is the best tool for opening oyster, but you can use any knife with a short, strong blade. Hold the shell, rounded side down, with a tea towel (dish towel) to protect your hand. Insert the blade of the knife between the shells near the hinge. Twist the knife to open the shell slightly, slide the blade towards the front of the oyster and sever the muscle. You can empty out the juices; if the oysters are very fresh, it will re-form.

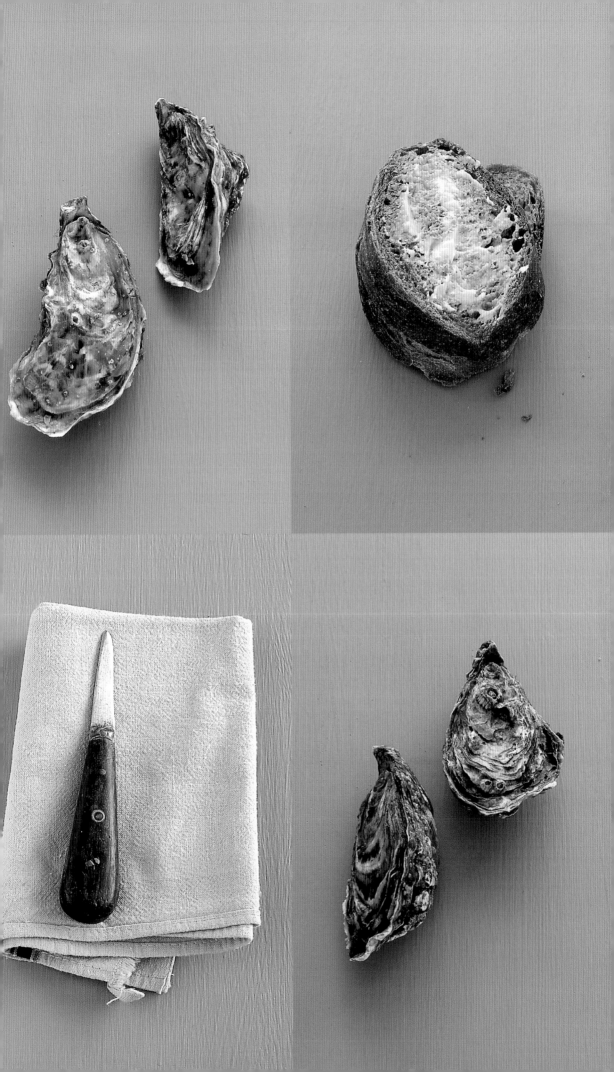

Small shellfish

Mussels

There are numerous kinds of mussels and cultivated mussels farmed on suspended ropes are particularly recommended. They can be stuffed, baked, sautéed, or even grilled (broiled).

Scrub mussels thoroughly under cold running water. Use a small knife to knock off any barnacles stuck to their shells and pull off the beards. Make sure you discard any that are broken or with holes in their shells, as well as any that do not shut immediately when sharply tapped with a knife. Mussels can be stored, wrapped in a damp tea towel (dish towel), in the bottom of the refrigerator for 24 hours; remove the beards and scrub them at the last moment.

The classic cooking method of cooking mussels involves sautéing them in a tightly covered pan until they open.

Mussels with lemon grass

Serves 4
Preparation: 20 minutes
Cooking: 15 minutes

4 spring onions (scallions), thinly sliced
1.5-cm/³⁄₄-inch piece of fresh root ginger, cut into thin batons
1 small fresh red chilli, deseeded and chopped
2 lemon grass stalks, thinly sliced
200 ml/7 fl oz canned coconut milk
1 kg/2 lb live mussels, beards removed and scrubbed
½ bunch of coriander (cilantro), finely chopped
salt and freshly ground black pepper

Place the spring onions (scallions), ginger, chilli and lemon grass in a large pan, pour in the coconut milk and bring to the boil. Lower the heat and simmer for 10 minutes. Add the mussels, cover tightly and cook, shaking the pan occasionally, for 3-5 minutes until the shells have opened. Discard any that remain closed. Remove the mussels with a slotted spoon and set aside in a warm serving dish. Boil the cooking juices until reduced by half. Strain, season with salt and pepper and pour over the mussels. Sprinkle with the coriander (cilantro), stir and serve immediately.

Tricks of the trade • These quantities are sufficient as an appetizer. If you want to serve the mussels as a main course, you'll need 500 g/1 lb per serving, that is a total of 2 kg/4 lb.

Mussels with Munster cheese

Serves 4
Preparation: 25 minutes
Cooking: 15 minutes

20 g/³⁄₄ oz/1½ tablespoons butter
2 shallots, thinly sliced
1 kg/1 lb live mussels, beards removed and scrubbed
350 ml/12 fl oz/1½ cups dry white wine
75 g/3 oz Munster cheese, thinly sliced
100 ml/3½ fl oz/scant ½ cup whipping cream
½ bunch of flat leaf parsley, finely chopped
salt and freshly ground black pepper

Melt the butter in a heavy-based pan, add the shallots, cover and cook over a low heat for about 5 minutes until soft. Add the mussels, white wine and a little pepper. Cover tightly and cook, shaking the pan occasionally, for 3-5 minutes, until the shells have opened. Discard any that remain closed. Remove the mussels with a slotted spoon and set aside in a warm serving dish. Boil the cooking juices until reduced by half, then strain into a clean pan. Add the cream and the cheese and melt over a low heat for 10 minutes, stirring constantly with a wooden spoon. Pour the sauce over the mussels, stir carefully and sprinkle with parsley before serving.

Tricks of the trade • These quantities are sufficient as an appetizer. If you want to serve the mussels as a main course, you'll need 500 g/1 lb per serving, that is a total of 2 kg/4 lb.

Mussels Provençal style

Serves 4
Preparation: 20 minutes
Cooking: 20 minutes

150 g/5 oz/generous ³⁄₄ cup diced smoked bacon
1 onion, cut into small wedges
1 garlic clove, chopped
1 red (bell) pepper, cut into small strips
2 tomatoes, skinned and diced
1 thyme sprig
1 bay leaf
2 kg/2 lb live mussels, beards removed and scrubbed
300 ml/½ pint/1¼ cups dry white wine
1 bunch of basil, finely chopped
salt and freshly ground black pepper

Place the bacon and onion in a heavy-based pan and cook over a medium heat, stirring occasionally, for 5 minutes. Add the garlic, red (bell) pepper, tomatoes, thyme and bay leaf. Season with salt pepper. Lower the heat, cover and cook, stirring occasionally, for 10 minutes.
Add the mussels and the white wine to the pan. Cover tightly and cook, shaking the pan occasionally, for 3-5 minutes until the shells have opened. Discard any that remain closed.
Just before serving, sprinkle with the basil and stir gently.

Mussels with cream and white wine

Serves 4
Preparation: 15 minutes
Cooking: 8 minutes

50 g/2 oz/¼ cup butter
2 shallots, thinly sliced
2 kg/2 lb live mussels, beards removed and scrubbed
1 thyme sprig
1 bay leaf
300 ml/½ pint/1¼ cups dry white wine
250 ml/8 fl oz/1 cup double (heavy) cream
1 bunch of flat leaf parsley, finely chopped
salt and freshly ground black pepper

Melt the butter in a heavy-based saucepan. Add the shallots, cover and cook over a low heat for about 5 minutes until softened. Add the mussels, thyme, bay leaf and white wine and season with pepper. Cover tightly and cook, shaking the pan occasionally, for 3-5 minutes until the shells have opened. Discard any that remain closed.
Remove the mussels, thyme and bay leaf with a slotted spoon. Set the mussels aside in a warm serving dish and discard the herbs. Add the cream to the cooking juices and bring to the boil, stirring constantly. Taste and adjust seasoning if necessary. Pour the cream sauce over the mussels, mix gently and sprinkle with the parsley before serving.

Cephalopods

Squid

Squid can be fried, sautéed or stuffed.

To prepare squid, pull off the head; the innards will come away with it. Cut off the tentacles and remove the beak. Discard the head. Cut the body sac in half, unless you want to stuff it, and rinse under cold running water to remove the slimy layer and the quill. Reserve the ink sac if it is required for the recipe. Finally, remove the outer membrane by rubbing with salt, or using a clean, soap-free scouring pad, then rinse again.

After you have cut the squid according to the recipe, it should be sautéed very quickly for 3–4 minutes to prevent it from becoming rubbery.

Cuttlefish

Prepare in exactly same way as squid, but instead of the quill, you'll find a hard structure called the cuttlebone.

Octopus

Octopus can be grilled (broiled), poached, sautéed, fried or steamed.

To prepare, cut off the tentacles and remove the beak by pushing it up and out through the centre of the tentacles. Turn the body inside out and discard the innards, except the ink sac if it is required for a recipe. Cut off and discard the portion containing the eyes. Wash very thoroughly.

To tenderize the flesh, pound with a meat mallet (bat) and/or blanch in boiling water.

The ink sac must be removed before cooking. You can keep it to make an excellent risotto nero.

Depending on their size, octopus should be cooked for 1–1½ hours. They must be very tender before you eat them.

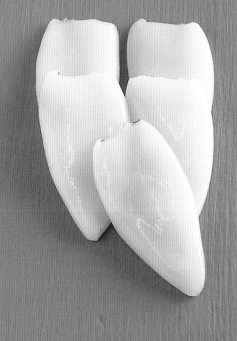

Stuffed squid

Serves 6
Preparation: 1 hour
Cooking: 30 minutes

300 g/10 oz small or medium-sized squid
4-cm/1¾-inch piece of fresh root ginger
2 tablespoons olive oil
150 g/5 oz/1¼ cups minced (ground) meat (eg lamb, beef or pork)
1 garlic clove, crushed
6 spring onions (scallions), thinly sliced
1 small fresh red chilli, deseeded and sliced
5 tablespoons soy sauce
1 teaspoon Thai fish sauce
200 ml/7 fl oz/scant 1 cup chicken stock
50 g/2 oz cellophane noodles
4 coriander (cilantro) sprigs, coarsely chopped
2 mint sprigs, coarsely chopped
2 Thai basil sprigs, coarsely chopped
1 tablespoon sesame oil
1 teaspoon caster (superfine) sugar

Clean the squid (see page 150), reserving the tentacles and keeping the body sacs whole. Chop the tentacles. Cut half the ginger into thin batons and grate the remainder.

Heat 1 tablespoon of the olive oil in a deep frying pan (skillet). Add the minced (ground) meat and cook, stirring frequently, until browned. Add the chopped tentacles, garlic, spring onions (scallions), the ginger batons, chilli, 1 tablespoon of the soy sauce and the Thai fish sauce. Stir well, cover and cook over a low heat for 10 minutes.

Meanwhile, bring the chicken stock to the boil, add the noodles and cook for 4 minutes, then drain, reserving the stock. Using a pair of kitchen scissors, cut the noodles into short lengths and add to the mixture in the frying pan (skillet).

Strain the stuffing mixture, pouring the cooking juices into the reserved chicken stock. Place the stuffing in a bowl and add the chopped herbs.

Mix well. Stuff the body sacs of the squid, no more than two-thirds full, and secure with a cocktail stick (toothpick). Prick the squid in several places with the point of a knife so that they don't burst during cooking.

Heat the remaining olive oil in a large, deep frying pan (skillet). Add the squid, in batches, and sauté for 3 minutes on each side until evenly browned. Arrange the stuffed squid on a large sheet of foil and drizzle with the reserved cooking juices. Fold up the sides and seal the foil into a parcel (package). Place on a baking (cookie) sheet and keep hot in a preheated oven, 150°C (300°F), gas mark 2.

Make a sauce by mixing together the remaining soy sauce, the sesame oil, sugar and the grated ginger in a bowl.

Serve the squid piping hot with the sauce or on its own with a well-seasoned salad.

Tricks of the trade • The difficult thing about this recipe is stuffing the squid – a funnel may be helpful.
Squid vary a great deal in size; you should reckon on about 3 or 4 small squid per person. The amount of stuffing given in this recipe is perfect for filling 25 small squid.
You'll find Thai basil in Asian food stores.

Salt-and-pepper
sautéed cuttlefish

Serves 6
Preparation: 25 minutes
Cooking: 8 minutes

750 g/1½ lb cuttlefish tubes
15 g/½ oz/1 tablespoon butter
2 tablespoons olive oil
3 garlic cloves, chopped
½ bunch of parsley, finely chopped
sea salt and freshly ground black pepper
To serve: green salad (salad greens)

Rinse the cuttlefish tubes under cold running water
and pat dry with kitchen paper (paper towels).
Cut them in half and score the flesh with a sharp
knife in a criss-cross pattern.
Heat half of the butter with 1 tablespoon of the
olive oil in a deep frying pan (skillet). Add half the
cuttlefish and half the garlic and season with
salt and pepper. Cook, stirring occasionally, for
3 minutes until well browned all over. Remove from
the pan and keep warm.
Wipe out the frying pan (skillet) with kitchen paper
(paper towels) and repeat the process with the
remaining butter, oil, cuttlefish and garlic.
Return the first batch of cuttlefish to the pan to
reheat, stir in the parsley and cook for a further
2 minutes.
Serve immediately with a well-seasoned green salad
(salad greens).

Tricks of the trade • Use very small cuttlefish for this recipe,
as their flesh is more tender and melt-in-the-mouth. You could
replace the garlic and parsley with 150 g/5 oz thinly sliced cho-
rizo and cook this at the same time as the cuttlefish tubes –
not in butter, but in 2 tablespoons olive oil. For this variation,
go easy on the salt and pepper.

Squid in its own ink with pasta

Serves 6
Preparation: 40 minutes
Cooking: 35 minutes

400 g/13 oz small squid
3 tablespoons olive oil
3 garlic cloves, chopped
1/2 bunch of flat leaf parsley, finely chopped
1 onion, thinly sliced
240-g/7 1/2 oz can chopped tomatoes
175 ml/6 fl oz/3/4 cup white wine
2 sachets (packets) squid ink
500 g/1 lb spaghettini
1/2 bunch of chives, finely chopped
salt and freshly ground black pepper

Clean the squid (see page 150), reserving the tentacles and keeping the body sacs whole. Slice the body sacs into thin rings.
Heat 2 tablespoons of the olive oil in a deep frying pan (skillet). Add all the squid and cook over a high heat for 2 minutes. Add the garlic and parsley and cook for a further 2 minutes. Remove the squid from the pan and keep warm.

Heat the remaining olive oil in a large flameproof casserole. Add the onion and cook over a high heat, stirring occasionally, for 5 minutes until browned. Add the tomatoes with the juice from the can and the white wine. Season with salt and pepper. Cover and cook over a low heat for 15 minutes. Stir in the squid ink, cover and cook for a further 5 minutes. Meanwhile, bring a large pan of salted water to the boil and cook the pasta for 2–3 minutes less than the packet instructions suggest. Stir 2 ladlefuls of the cooking water from the pasta into the sauce, then drain the pasta and add to the sauce with the squid. Stir well and cook over a low heat, stirring constantly, for 2-3 minutes.
Taste and adjust the seasoning, if necessary, and serve immediately, sprinkled chives.

Tricks of the trade • You'll find sachets (packets) of squid ink at your fish suppliers and at some supermarkets. Alternatively, if you buy your squid whole and unprepared, save the ink sacs and collect the ink by placing the sacs in a strainer over a bowl and crushing them with a small spoon.

Small crustaceans

Shrimp, prawns and king prawns (jumbo shrimp)

Note that in the UK, the term shrimp refers to small crustaceans and larger ones are called prawns. In the United States, they are all called shrimp, regardless of a size. Whatever size prawns (shrimp) you're using, you must make sure that they're fresh. If you are buying them ready-cooked, their tails should be curled in towards their bodies, proof that they were alive at the time of cooking.

The simplest way of cooking these small crustaceans is to plunge them into very salty boiling water for 2–3 minutes. If you can cook them in unpolluted sea water, so much the better. Enjoy them while they are still hot. King prawns (jumbo shrimp), also known as Mediterranean prawns, should be pan-fried for 2 minutes on each side.

Peeling them is easy: pull off the head, then remove the shell enclosing the body and pull gently on the tail to remove any remaining shell in one piece. Finally, devein by making a shallow incision along the back and pull out the thin black thread. You can save the heads and shells to prepare a stock.

Tricks of the trade • If you can't find any raw prawns (shrimp), here's a little trick for freshening-up cooked specimens: bring a saucepan of water to the boil with a handful of coarse salt, 1 teaspoon freshly ground black pepper, 1 bay leaf and 3 thyme sprigs. Tip the prawns (shrimp) into a strainer or colander, pour the boiling water over them, drain and serve immediately, sprinkled with a pinch of sea salt.

Langoustines

Only buy live langoustines and reject any whose tails are beginning to turn black and whose heads are coming off of their own accord. Choose them all of the same size, depending on the recipe. Smaller specimens are best for cooking in court-bouillon and larger ones for grilling (broiling). Langoustines are also known as Dublin Bay prawns, scampi and Norway lobster.

If you are not cooking them straight away, keep them in a container covered with clingfilm (plastic wrap) in the refrigerator, but they will not keep long.

The simplest way to cook langoustines is to plunge them into a very large pan of salted boiling water to which some pepper and the rind of a lemon have been added. They will be cooked as soon as the water comes back to the boil, at which point they should be removed. You can also grill (broil) them. Cut the in half, brush with butter and seasonings and grill (broil) for 4–5 minutes.

To peel them, separate the head from the thorax, snip open the belly with a pair of scissors, pull out the flesh and remove the long black thread with the tip of a knife. Once cooked they should be eaten without delay because they won't stand up to further chilling.

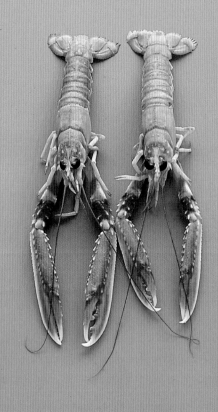

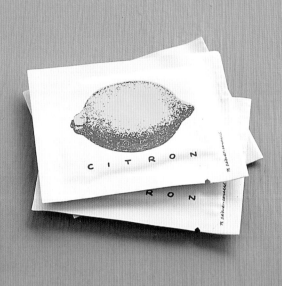

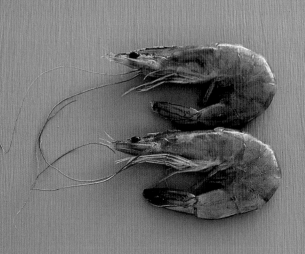

Brown shrimp with thyme

Serves 4
Preparation: 1 minute
Cooking: 3 minutes

3 fresh thyme sprigs
1 bay leaf
5 handfuls of coarse salt
2 tablespoons peppercorns
750 g/1½ lb raw brown shrimp
To serve: buttered brown bread

Bring 3 litres/5¼ pints/13 cups water to the boil
with the thyme, bay leaf, salt and peppercorns.
Tip the shrimp into the boiling water and cook for
3 minutes. Drain well on kitchen paper (paper
towels) and eat immediately with buttered brown
bread … yum!

Prawn (shrimp) tempura

Serves 4
Preparation: 40 minutes
Cooking: 15 minutes

125 g/4 oz/1 cup plain all-purpose flour, plus extra
for dredging
2 eggs
1 teaspoon salt
2 tablespoons groundnut (peanut) oil
150 ml/¼ pint/²⁄₃ cup beer
1 teaspoon cayenne pepper
10 coriander (cilantro) sprigs, finely chopped
1.5 litres/2½ pints/6¼ cups grapeseed oil
20 raw king prawns (jumbo shrimp), peeled and deveined
To serve: sweet-and-sour sauce

To prepare the tempura batter, place the flour in
a bowl, make a well in the centre and add the eggs,
groundnut (peanut) oil and salt. Mix with a wooden
spoon, then gradually blend in the beer a little at
a time. Add the cayenne pepper and coriander
(cilantro). Cover the bowl with a tea towel (dish
towel) and leave to rest for 2 hours.
Heat the grapeseed oil in a deep-fryer or wok.
Dredge the prawns (shrimp) in flour, shaking off any
excess. Grasping each prawn (shrimp) by the tail,
dip it in the tempura batter, then deep-fry in small
batches for about 2 minutes until golden brown.
Drain on kitchen paper (paper towels).
Wrap in foil and keep warm in a preheated oven,
150°C (300°F), gas mark 2, while you cook the
other batches.
Serve hot with the sweet-and-sour sauce.

Scampi fritti

Serves 4
Preparation: 20 minutes
Cooking: 10 minutes per batch
Resting: 2 hours

750 g/1½ lb large langoustines
250 g/8 oz/2 cups plain (all-purpose) flour, plus extra
for dredging
3 eggs
3 tablespoons groundnut (peanut) oil
1 teaspoon salt
250 ml/8 fl oz/1 cup beer
2 limes, cut into wedges
vegetable oil for deep-frying

To prepare the batter, place the flour in a bowl, make
a well in the centre and add the eggs, groundnut
(peanut) oil and salt. Mix with a wooden spoon, then
gradually blend in the beer a little at a time. Cover
the bowl with a tea towel (dish towel) and leave to
rest for 2 hours.
Heat the vegetable oil in a deep-fryer (it's best
to use one for this recipe). Peel the langoustines
and dredge them in flour, shaking off any excess.
Dip them in the batter and lower them into the
deep-fryer. Fry them in several batches.
Once the langoustines are golden brown, remove
and drain on kitchen paper (paper towels) and
keep them warm on a baking (cookie) sheet in a preheated oven, 150°C (300°F), gas mark 2.
When they are all cooked, serve hot with lime wedges. You could also hand round a homemade tartare
sauce.

Variation • You could also make this recipe with king prawns
(jumbo shrimp). Peel them before deep-frying. They take
almost exactly the same length of time to cook as the langoustines.

Prawns (shrimp) with ginger

Serves 4
Preparation: 5 minutes
Cooking: 3 minutes

20 g/³/₄ oz/1½ tablespoons butter
625 g1¼ lb raw prawns (shrimp), peeled and deveined
4-cm/1³/₄-inch piece of fresh root ginger, cut into thin batons
1 tablespoon sugar
freshly ground black pepper
To serve: herb salad (see page 184)

Melt the butter in a deep frying pan (skillet) and tip in the prawns (shrimp) and ginger. Add the sugar and season with pepper. Sauté over a high heat for 3 minutes, shaking the pan several times. Serve immediately with herb salad.

Variation • You can make this recipe with cooked peeled prawns. Tip them into the frying pan (skillet) 2 minutes after the ginger and sauté them for 1 minute only.

King prawns (jumbo shrimp) in red curry

Serves 6
Preparation: 40 minutes
Cooking: 20 minutes
Marinating: 30 minutes

3 tablespoons light soy sauce
2 tablespoons oyster sauce
12 large raw king prawns (jumbo shrimp), peeled and deveined
150 ml/5 fl oz/²/₃ cup canned coconut milk
1 teaspoon caster (superfine) sugar
freshly ground black pepper
To serve: cardamom rice (see page 186)

FOR THE RED CURRY PASTE:
1 fresh red chilli, deseeded
1 shallot, thinly sliced
1 lemon grass stalk, chopped
1 kaffir lime leaf, torn into pieces
1 coriander (cilantro) root
3 peppercorns
½ teaspoon coriander seeds
½ teaspoon cumin seeds
½ teaspoon ground turmeric
½ teaspoon shrimp paste
pinch of ground cinnamon
1 tablespoon groundnut (peanut) oil

Mix together the light soy sauce and oyster sauce in a shallow dish and season with a little pepper. Add the prawns (shrimp) and leave in a cool place to marinate for 30 minutes.
Place all the ingredients for the red curry paste except for the oil in a mortar and pound with a pestle to a smooth paste. Gradually work in the oil.
Place the prawns (shrimp) on a grill (broiler) rack and cook under a preheated grill (broiler) for 5 minutes, then turn and cook for a further 3 minutes.

Meanwhile, bring the coconut milk to the boil in a pan and stir in the red curry paste and sugar. Cook for 10 minutes over a low heat.
Serve the prawns (shrimp) immediately, drizzled with the sauce and accompanied by cardamom rice.

Langoustines with basil

Serves 4
Preparation: 20 minutes
Cooking: 8 minutes

16 large raw langoustines, halved lengthways and deveined
100 g/3½ oz/scant ½ cup butter
8 leaves basil, finely chopped
freshly ground black pepper

Arrange the langoustines on a baking (cookie) sheet lined with foil. Melt the butter in a small pan over a low heat with the basil and a pinch pepper. Drizzle the basil butter over the langoustines and cook under a preheated grill (broiler) for 8 minutes.
Serve the langoustines piping hot. Take care not to burn your fingers or mouth – and don't forget the napkins and finger bowls!

Prawns (shrimp) sautéed with coriander (cilantro)

Serves 4
Preparation: 30 minutes
Cooking: 5 minutes

1 tablespoon soy sauce
5 tablespoons extra virgin olive oil
20 large raw prawns (shrimp), peeled and deveined
½ bunch fresh coriander (cilantro), finely chopped
2 handfuls of rocket (arugula)
sea salt and freshly ground black pepper

Make a dressing by mixing together the soy sauce and 4 tablespoons of the olive oil in a bowl and seasoning to taste with salt and pepper.
Heat the remaining olive oil in a frying pan (skillet), tilting the pan to spread the oil evenly. Add the prawns (shrimp) and cook over a high heat for 2 minutes on each side. Add the coriander (cilantro) and season with salt and pepper. Cook for a few seconds more.
Toss the rocket (arugula) in the dressing and serve immediately with the warm prawns (shrimp).

Prawns (shrimp) and lemon grass soup

Serves 4
Preparation: 30 minutes
Cooking: 30 minutes
Marinating: 30 minutes minimum

16 large raw prawns (shrimp), peeled and deveined, heads and shells reserved
4 tablespoons lemon juice
4 kaffir lime leaves
1 fresh galangal root, thinly sliced
3 stalks fresh lemon grass, cut into short lengths
4 small fresh red chillies, halved and deseeded
4 spring onions (scallions), white parts thinly sliced and green parts cut into short lengths
300 g/10 oz button (white) mushrooms
2 tablespoons Thai fish sauce
3 tablespoons lime juice
½ bunch of coriander (cilantro), finely chopped
salt and freshly ground black pepper

Place the prawns (shrimp) on a plate, sprinkle with half the lemon juice and season with salt and pepper. Cover with clingfilm (plastic wrap) and set aside to marinate in a cool place for 1 hour.

Put the reserved heads and shells into a pan and pour in 750 ml/1¼ pints/3 cups water. Bring to the boil and add the kaffir lime leaves, galangal, lemon grass, 3 of the chillies and the white parts of the spring onions (scallions). Lower the heat and leave to simmer for 20 minutes.

Meanwhile, cut the mushrooms into quarters, place in a bowl and drizzle with the remaining lemon juice to prevent discoloration. Pound the remaining chilli in a mortar with a pestle.

Strain the stock and return it to the pan. Add the Thai fish sauce, lime juice and mushrooms. Simmer gently for 5 minutes. Check the seasoning and add the pounded chilli to taste.

Tip the prawns (shrimp) into the hot soup and cook over a medium heat for a further 2 minutes.

Serve immediately, sprinkled with coriander (cilantro) and the green parts of the spring onions (scallions).

Tricks of the trade • You could prepare everything a day ahead, then reheat the stock and cook the prawns (shrimp) at the last moment.

The prawns (shrimp) should be marinated for at least 30 minutes, but you could, of course, leave them in a cool place for longer if necessary.

For a sweeter version of this recipe, add 150 ml/¼ pint/⅔ cup canned coconut milk to the stock at the same time as the Thai fish sauce, lime juice and mushrooms. In this case, make the stock with only 500 ml/17 fl oz/generous 2 cups water, rather than 750 ml/1¼ pints/3 cups.

The king of crustaceans

Lobster

When buying lobster, make sure that it is lively as well as alive – moving about, its tail folded under its body, its shell and all its limbs hard and intact.

Choose several 400-500 g/13–16 oz lobsters in preference to one large one. The females have less meat in their legs than the males, but they may have coral (roe) which can be used as the basis for delicious sauces.

The classic way to kill and cook a lobster is to plunge it headfirst into boiling water, then cook it for about 12 minutes. Ideally you should cook it in unpolluted sea water, but nowadays most supermarkets sell coarse sea salt which you can add to ordinary tap water.

Another technique is to cut the lobster in half lengthways, then grill (broil) it for 12–15 minutes. Those who are squeamish, can always boil it for several seconds first. An alternative, recommended as more humane, is to place it in a plastic bag in the freezer for 2 hours.

Before grasping it (just behind the head with your thumb and index finger), make sure that its claws are tightly bound.

To prepare the cooked meat, first remove the head. with a pair of scissors, make a cut in the middle of the belly, open up the shell and gently pull the meat out in a single piece. Remove and discard the transparent stomach sac from just behind the head and the thin black intestine that runs the length of the body.

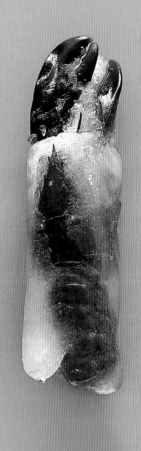

Lobsters boiled in sea water

Serves 4
Preparation: 25 minutes
Cooking: 12 minutes

4 litres/7 pints/17½ cups unpolluted seawater, strained, or fresh water mixed with 4 tablespoons coarse sea salt
4 live lobsters, about 400 g/12 oz each
50 g/2 oz/¼ cup butter
2 tablespoons lemon juice
freshly ground black pepper
To serve: steamed potatoes

Bring the water to the boil in a large pan and plunge the lobsters in head first. Cover and cook 12 minutes. Lift out, drain and leave until cool enough to handle. Meanwhile, melt the butter in a small pan with the lemon juice and a little pepper. Break off the lobsters' heads, cut off the claws and reserve them. Cut open the shells with a pair of scissors and lift out the tail meat in a single piece. Remove and discard the stomach sacs and intestines. Serve the meat drizzled with the lemon butter and accompanied by steamed potatoes. Crack the claws and offer them separately.

Variation • You could also eat the lobster cold, with a good homemade mayonnaise (see page 178).

Lobsters in a lemon grass court-bouillon

Serves 4
Preparation: 30 minutes
Cooking: 25 minutes

2 live lobsters, about 625 g/1¼ lb each
1 thyme sprig
1 bay leaf
2 lemon grass stalks, split in half
pinch of saffron
1 leek, cut into chunks
2 carrots, cut into chunks
sea salt and freshly ground black pepper

Bring a large pan of salted water to the boil. Plunge in the lobsters head first and cook for 5 minutes. Lift out, drain, and leave to cool.
Pour 1.2 litres/2 pints/5 cups water into a pan and add salt and pepper, the thyme sprig, bay leaf, lemon grass stalks and saffron. Bring to the boil and add the leek and carrots. Cook for 10 minutes.
Meanwhile, shell the lobsters: break off the heads, cut off and reserve the claws. Make a cut in the middle of the belly with a pair of scissors, open the shell and remove the meat in a single piece. Discard the stomach sac and black intestine. Cut the tail meat into several chunks, then crack open the claws and pick out the meat. Add the meat to the court-bouillon and continue cooking for 8 minutes more. Remove and discard the thyme sprig and bay leaf before serving in deep soup plates.

Grilled (broiled) 'red' lobsters

Serves 4
Preparation: 20 minutes
Cooking: 12 minutes

2 live female lobsters, 400-500 g/13–16 oz each
20 g butter, melted
150 ml/¼ pint/⅔ cup crème fraîche or soured (sour) cream
pinch of saffron
salt and freshly ground black pepper

Cut the lobsters in half lengthways. If you prefer, you can first place them in the freezer for 2 hours or plunge them head first into a large pan of salted, boiling water for 2 minutes (see page 168). Discard the stomach sacs and intestines and reserve the juices, tomalley (liver) and coral (roe).
Generously brush the lobster meat with melted butter and place on a baking (cookie) sheet, shell side down. Cook under a preheated grill (broiler) for about 12 minutes. The lobsters are cooked when their flesh has turned opaque.
Meanwhile, pound the the tomalley and coral with the reserved juices in a mortar with a pestle. Spoon into a heatproof bowl and stir in the crème fraîche or cream and saffron and season with a pinch each of salt and pepper. Set over a pan of gently simmering water.
Serve the lobsters drizzled with the red sauce, or serve the sauce separately.

Vastly improved bisque

Serves 4
Preparation: 20 minutes
Cooking: 10 minutes

1 cooked lobster
750 ml/1¼ pints/3 cups ready-made lobster bisque
50 g/2 oz/⅔ cup Parmesan cheese shavings
12 croûtons
olive oil, for drizzling
½ bunch of chives, finely chopped

Shell the lobster: break off the head and remove and reserve the claws. Make a cut in the middle of its belly with a pair of kitchen scissors, then open the shell and remove the meat in a single piece. Remove and discard the stomach sac and black intestine. Cut the tail meat into several chunks, then crack open the claws and pick out the meat. Heat the bisque in a large saucepan. Divide the lobster meat among 4 shallow bowls, and sprinkle with the Parmesan and croûtons. Pour over the piping hot lobster bisque, drizzle with some olive oil and sprinkle with finely chopped chives.

Tricks of the trade • Freshly cooked lobsters are widely available, especially in coastal towns. Choose a good-quality lobster bisque from a delicatessen and be prepared to pay that little extra for it.

Other crustaceans

Velvet swimming crabs

To some gourmets these are far and away the finest-tasting crabs. Always choose live ones, heavy but not too big. Plunge them into boiling court-bouillon and cook for 10–15 minutes, according to their size, timing them from when the liquid returns to the boil. To prepare the crabs, pull off the top part of the shell and cut the crab in two. Lay the pieces out horizontally and, using a well-sharpened knife, cut the crab between its legs: this will allow you to extract the maximum amount of meat. Crack the claws and pick out the meat.

Crabs

Choose live crabs and note that the shell should be dirty. Select females for preference. Weigh the crab in your hand; it should feel heavy and quite full. To cook and prepare them, proceed as for the velvet swimming crabs, but cook for 25 minutes in the court-bouillon.

Sea urchins

Sea urchins are eaten raw, but first of all you have to open them! If you are right-handed, take them in your (well-protected) left hand, and, with a pair of small, sharp scissors, pierce the soft part next to the mouth, then cut out a lid. You then need only lift out the corals with a little spoon held upside down (rounded part up) to avoid pulling out the blackish threads.

Spider crabs

Spider crabs should be bought live. The heavier they are, the better they'll be. Choose females for preference: they are finer-tasting. Cook them in boiling court-bouillon for 25 minutes, timing them from when the liquid comes back to the boil. Spider crabs are best eaten hot. To prepare them, cut the abdomen in half from top to bottom, then cut each half in half again, still in the same direction. Next, twist each leg off the abdomen. Use a long, pointed tool to dig the meat out of the legs.

Crab dressed in olive oil and lemon

Serves 4
Preparation: 40 minutes
Cooking: 25 minutes

3 litres/5¼ pints/13 cups court-bouillon with (hard) cider (see page 16)
2 live crabs, about 1 kg/2 lb each
125 ml/4 fl oz/½ cup olive oil
6 tablespoons lemon juice
1 lettuce, torn into pieces
salt and freshly ground black pepper

Bring the court-bouillon to the boil in a large pan. Plunge in the crabs and cook for 25 minutes, timing them from when the liquid returns to the boil. Lift them out and leave them to cool.
Meanwhile, mix together the olive oil and lemon juice in a bowl and season with salt and pepper. Extract the meat from the crabs (see page 172). Toss the lettuce with half the dressing and divide among 4 plates. Place the crab meat on each plate next to the salad and drizzle everything with the remaining dressing.

Spider crab mayonnaise

Serves 4
Preparation: 50 minutes (for the court-bouillon)
Cooking: 25 minutes

3 litres/5¼ pints/13 cups classic court-bouillon (see page 16)
4 very heavy female spider crabs
To serve: mayonnaise (see page 178)

Bring the court-bouillon to the boil in a large pan. Plunge in the crabs and cook for 25 minutes, timing them from when the liquid returns to the boil. Lift them out and extract the meat (see page 172). Serve immediately, accompanied by a good home-made mayonnaise.

Sea urchins in their shells

Serves 6
Preparation: 30 minutes
Cooking: 8 minutes

12 sea urchins
6 eggs
40 g/1½ oz/3 tablespoons butter
salt and freshly ground black pepper
To serve: buttered baguette slices

Open the sea urchins (see page 172). Cut out a wide
lid one-third of the way down each urchin and
remove the corals.
Clean the inside of 6 sea urchin shells and discard
the remainder. Take care not to hurt yourself!
Divide half the coral among the 6 reserved shells
and break 1 egg into each. Add a knob (pat) of
butter and season with salt and pepper.
Transfer to a baking (cookie) sheet and bake in a
preheated oven, 240°C (475°F). gas mark 9, for
8 minutes.
As soon as they're cooked, divide the remaining
coral among the shells and serve immediately with
slices of buttered baguette to use as dippers.

Accompaniments

hollandaise sauce

glutinous rice

ratatouille

mayonnaise

crushed potatoes

rouille

Beurre noisette (brown butter)

Serves 4
Preparation: 25 minutes
Cooking: 3 minutes

150 g/5 oz/⅔ cup butter, cut into pieces
1 tablespoon lemon juice
salt and freshly ground black pepper

Melt the butter over a low heat without stirring. Skim off the foam that forms on the surface. Pour the clarified butter into a bowl, taking care to leave behind the whitish milk solids that have settled on the base of the pan. Heat the clarified butter in a clean pan until it turns golden brown. Season with salt and pepper and add the lemon juice. Serve very hot as an accompaniment to grilled (broiled) fish.

Vanilla beurre blanc

Serves 4
Preparation: 10 minutes
Cooking: 15 minutes

5 shallots, finely chopped
2 tablespoons white wine vinegar
4 tablespoons white wine
250 g/8 oz/1 cup cold butter, cut into small pieces
2 vanilla pods (beans), slit open, seeds scraped out
salt and freshly ground black pepper

Place the shallots, vinegar and white wine in a pan over a medium heat and cook, stirring constantly, for about 5 minutes until almost all the liquid has reduced. Whisk in the butter, a piece at a time, then add the seeds from the vanilla pods (beans). Season with salt and pepper and serve.

Hollandaise sauce

Serves 4
Preparation: 20 minutes
Cooking: 15 minutes

2 egg yolks
2 tablespoons lemon juice
125 g/4 oz/½ cup cold butter, cut into small pieces
salt and freshly ground black pepper

Put the egg yolks and lemon juice in the top of a double boiler or a heatproof bowl and season with salt and pepper. Set over a pan of barely simmering water and whisk until the mixture thickens. Add the butter, whisking constantly. If you're not serving the hollandaise at once, leave it over the warm water but turn off the heat. This is the perfect accompaniment for fish poached in court-bouillon.

Variations • Add a teaspoon of caviar just before serving. To lighten the sauce, whisk the two egg whites until stiff and gently fold into the warm hollandaise.

Mayonnaise

Serves 4–6
Preparation: 15 minutes

2 egg yolks, at room temperature
2 teaspoons Dijon or other mustard
250 ml/8 fl oz/1 cup olive oil
1 teaspoon white wine vinegar
salt and freshly ground black pepper

Whisk together the egg yolks and mustard in a bowl and season with salt and pepper. Add the oil drop by drop, whisking vigorously. When half the oil has been added, whisk in the vinegar, then continue adding the olive oil in a thin trickle, whisking constantly. Taste and adjust the seasoning if necessary.

Rouille

Serves 6
Preparation: 25 minutes

5 garlic cloves, halved
2 small red chillies, deseeded and chopped
2 egg yolks
250 ml/8 fl oz/1 cup olive oil
salt and freshly ground black pepper

Put the garlic and chillies in a mortar and pound to a smooth paste with a pestle. Transfer to a bowl and whisk in the egg yolks. Season with salt and a little pepper. Add the oil drop by drop, whisking vigorously. This very spicy condiment is the traditional accompaniment for fish soup or bouillabaisse.
Use with caution. Aïoli is prepared in the same way, but without the chilli and with more pepper.

Tarragon beurre blanc

Serves 4
Preparation: 10 minutes
Cooking: 20 minutes

3 shallots, finely chopped
1 tablespoon white wine vinegar
100 ml/3½ fl oz/scant ½ cup white wine
250 g/8 oz/1 cup cold butter, cut into small pieces
2 tablespoons warm water
5 tarragon sprigs, finely chopped
salt and freshly ground black pepper

Put the shallots, vinegar and white wine in a pan and cook over a medium heat for about 10 minutes until almost all of the liquid has reduced. Whisk in the butter, a piece at a time, then whisk in the warm water and tarragon. Season with salt and pepper and serve immediately.

Tricks of the trade • If you're concerned that your beurre blanc won't come out well, try making it over a saucepan of simmering water. Tarragon beurre blanc is delicious, but you can also flavour this sauce just as successfully with mint, basil, parsley, sorrel or dill.

Kikine's sauce

Serves 6
Preparation: 15 minutes
Marinating: 1 hour

2 tomatoes
2 tablespoons balsamic vinegar
1 bunch of basil
100 ml/3½ fl oz/scant ½ cup olive oil
salt and freshly ground black pepper

Place the tomatoes in a bowl and cover with boiling water. Leave for 1–2 minutes, drain, cut a cross at the stem end of each tomato and peel off the skins. Halve, deseed and chop finely. Place the chopped tomato in a bowl, add the vinegar and set aside in a cool place for 1 hour to marinate. Put the basil leaves and olive oil in a food processor and season with salt and pepper Pulse several times to blend, pour into a bowl and stir in the marinated tomatoes. Serve with grilled (broiled) fish.

Salsa verde

Serves 6
Preparation: 15 minutes

2 tablespoons white wine vinegar
5 tablespoons olive oil
⅓ bunch of chervil, finely chopped
⅓ bunch of flat leaf parsley, finely chopped
⅓ bunch of tarragon, finely chopped
1 handful of rocket (arugula) or watercress, finely chopped
⅓ bunch of chives, finely chopped
4 hard-boiled (hard-cooked) eggs, mashed
5 small gherkins (dill pickles), diced
1 tablespoon capers, rinsed
salt and freshly ground black pepper

Pour the vinegar and olive oil into a bowl and season with salt and pepper. Stir, then add the herbs, rocket (arugula) or watercress, eggs, gherkins (pickles) and capers. Serve with cold or poached fish.

Ginger cream sauce

Serves 4
Preparation: 5 minutes
Cooking: 15 minutes

250 ml/8 fl oz/1 cup double (heavy) cream
4-cm/1¾-inch piece of fresh root ginger, chopped
salt and freshly ground black pepper

Heat the cream and ginger in a pan over a medium heat for 15 minutes, but do not boil. Strain, season with salt and pepper and serve with poached or steamed fish, or fish baked in parcels (packages).

Variation • You could infuse (steep) the cream with 2 split lemon grass stalks or even some crushed garlic. The flavours remain very subtle and combine deliciously with the taste of the fish. Whichever seasoning you use, make sure you strain the cream sauce before serving it.

Sauce vierge

Serves 6
Preparation: 15 minutes
Marinating: 2 hours

4 tomatoes
2 garlic cloves, finely chopped
½ bunch of chives, chopped
3 tarragon sprigs, chopped
10 basil leaves, chopped
4 tablespoons lemon juice
250 ml/8 fl oz/1 cup olive oil
salt and freshly ground black pepper

Place the tomatoes in a bowl and cover with boiling water. Leave for 1–2 minutes, then drain, cut a cross at the stem end of each tomato and peel off the skins. Halve and deseed. Mix together the tomatoes, garlic, herbs, lemon juice and oil in a bowl, then season with salt and pepper. Leave to stand for 2 hours to allow the flavours to mingle before serving with poached or steamed fish.

Butter with olive oil and lemon

Serves 4
Preparation: 5 minutes
Cooking: 5 minutes

100 g/3½ oz/scant ½ cup butter, cut into pieces
3 tablespoons olive oil
2 tablespoons lemon juice
freshly ground black pepper

Place the butter, olive oil and lemon juice in a microwave-safe bowl and season with pepper. Microwave on medium for 2 minutes.
Alternatively, heat the mixture in a pan over a low heat for 5 minutes.
Serve piping hot as an accompaniment to poached or steamed fish.

Olive oil with fennel seeds

Serves 4
Preparation: 5 minutes

6 tablespoons olive oil
2 tablespoons lemon juice
1 tablespoon fennel seeds
salt and freshly ground black pepper

Combine all the ingredients in a bowl and season with salt and pepper. Serve with grilled (broiled) fish.

Thalie's ratatouille

Serves 6–8
Preparation: 30 minutes
Cooking: 4 hours

3 tablespoons olive oil
3 onions, cut into wedges
400-g/13-oz can tomatoes
6 courgettes (zucchini), coarsely diced
1 small aubergine (eggplant), cut into chunks
½ teaspoon ground cumin
½ bunch of coriander (cilantro), coarsely chopped
½ teaspoon paprika
6 red, yellow or orange (bell) peppers
salt and freshly ground black pepper

Heat the olive oil in a large pan. Add the onions and cook over a high heat, stirring occasionally, for 5 minutes until golden.

Add the tomatoes and their can juice, courgettes (zucchini) and aubergine (eggplant). Season with salt and pepper and add the cumin, coriander (cilantro) and paprika. Cover and cook over a very low heat for 2 hours.

Meanwhile, place the (bell) peppers under a preheated grill (broiler), turning occasionally, until they are charred and blistered all over. Using tongs, transfer them to a plastic bag, seal the top and leave to cool. When they are cool enough to handle, peel off their skins. Halve and deseed, then cut the flesh into strips.

When the ratatouille has been cooking for 2 hours, add the sliced (bell) peppers and cook, uncovered, for a further 2 hours. Check the ratatouille frequently and remove from the heat if it begins to scorch. Taste and adjust the seasoning if necessary. Serve hot or cold.

Lemon-braised chicory (Belgian endive)

Serves 4
Preparation: 10 minutes
Cooking: 25 minutes

8 chicory (Belgian endive) heads
50 g/2 oz/¼ cup butter
2 tablespoons olive oil
2 tablespoons caster (superfine) sugar
2 tablespoons lemon juice
salt and freshly ground black pepper

Trim the chicory (Belgian endive) and remove the bitter core at the base of each head. Steam for 20 minutes.

Melt the butter with the olive oil in a large, deep frying pan (skillet). Add the chicory (Belgian endive), sprinkle with the sugar and season with salt and pepper. Cook over a high heat for 3 minutes, turning halfway through cooking. Drizzle with the lemon juice and serve immediately.

Spiced sautéed courgettes (zucchini)

Serves 4
Preparation: 10 minutes
Cooking: 10 minutes

2 tablespoons olive oil
4 courgettes (zucchini), diced
¼ teaspoon grated nutmeg
¼ teaspoon ground cinnamon
¼ teaspoon ground cloves
¼ teaspoon black pepper
sea salt

Heat the olive oil in a large, deep frying pan (skillet). Add the courgettes (zucchini) and cook, stirring frequently for 5–10 minutes until lightly browned all over. (They should be crisp but tender.) Season with the spices and salt and serve immediately.

Crushed potatoes

Serves 6
Preparation: 30 minutes
Cooking: 15 minutes

1 kg/2 lb waxy potatoes

OLIVE OIL VERSION:
100 ml/3½ fl oz/scant ½ cup olive oil
sea salt and freshly ground black pepper

BUTTERED VERSION:
150 g/5 oz/⅔ cup butter, softened
4 tablespoons lemon juice
⅓ bunch of flat leaf parsley, finely chopped
freshly ground black pepper

Cook the potatoes in salted, boiling water for 15 minutes. Pierce with the point of a knife to check they are tender. Drain and transfer to a large plate. For the olive oil version: crush the potatoes with a fork, gradually blending in the olive oil, then season with salt and pepper.

For the buttered version: crush the potatoes with a fork, gradually blending in the softened butter and lemon juice, then season with pepper and sprinkle with the parsley.

Either way, the potatoes are delicious and they make a perfect accompaniment for fish.

Tricks of the trade • Never use the blender for this dish. It takes a bit longer with a fork, but preserves the texture of the potatoes, rather than reducing everything to a smooth pap. Use high-quality raw materials; a really good olive oil will work wonders with this seemingly ordinary dish.

Braised leeks with butter

Serves 4
Preparation: 5 minutes
Cooking: 15 minutes

750 g/1½ lb baby leeks, white parts only
50 g/2 oz/¼ cup butter
sea salt and freshly ground black pepper

Steam the leeks for 10 minutes. Drain well on kitchen paper (paper towels).
Melt the butter in a large, deep frying pan (skillet) and add the leeks in a single layer. Cook over a medium heat for 2 minutes on each side. Season with salt and pepper and serve immediately.

Herb salad

Serves 6
Preparation: 15 minutes

3 tablespoons lime juice
3 tablespoons olive oil
1 tablespoon soy sauce (optional)
300 g/10 oz mesclun
½ bunch of coriander (cilantro), leaves only
½ bunch of chervil, leaves only
3 tarragon sprigs, leaves only
3 flat leaf parsley sprigs, leaves only
½ bunch of chives, finely chopped
a few basil leaves
sea salt and freshly ground black pepper

Mix together the lime juice, olive oil and soy sauce in a salad bowl. Add the mesclun, and the coriander (cilantro), chervil, parsley, tarragon, chives and basil. Season with salt and pepper. Set aside in a cool place and toss the salad just before serving.
You could also add some thinly shaved Parmesan cheese, confit, chopped sun-dried tomatoes or a few pine nuts, to name just a few alternatives.

Tricks of the trade • Go easy on the salt if you are adding soya (soy) sauce to the dressing.

Green beans with coriander (cilantro)

Serves 6
Preparation: 20 minutes
Cooking: 12 minutes

1.25 kg/2½ lb green beans
olive oil, for drizzling
½ bunch of coriander (cilantro), finely chopped
sea salt and freshly ground black pepper

Bring a large pan of salted water to the boil. Add the green beans, lower the heat and simmer them gently for 12 minutes.
Drain the beans and place them on a large dish. Drizzle with the olive oil, sprinkle with the coriander (cilantro) and season with salt and pepper. Serve immediately.

Oven-roasted tomatoes with basil

Serves 6
Preparation: 20 minutes
Resting: 30 minutes
Cooking: 2 hours 30 minutes

12 vine tomatoes
2 tablespoons olive oil, plus extra for brushing and drizzling
1 tablespoon tomato purée (paste)
2 garlic cloves, finely chopped
15 basil leaves
½ teaspoon ground cumin
2 tablespoons caster (superfine) sugar
salt and freshly ground black pepper

Halve and deseed the tomatoes, then leave them to drain upside down on kitchen paper (paper towels).
Mix together the olive oil, tomato purée (paste), garlic, basil and cumin in a bowl.
Brush a baking (cookie) sheet with olive oil and arrange the tomatoes on it cut side up.
Using a small spoon, place a little of the tomato purée (paste) herb and oil mixture on top of each tomato. Drizzle with more olive oil, season with pepper and sprinkle with the sugar. Bake in a preheated oven, 150°C (300°F), gas mark 2, for 2½ hours.

Cardamom rice

Serves 6
Preparation: 5 minutes
Cooking: 15 minutes

3 cups basmati rice
1 tablespoon olive oil
3 split cardamom pods
salt and freshly ground black pepper

Wash the rice in several changes of water until the water runs clear.
Pour 1.5 litres/2½ pints/6 cups water into a pan, add a pinch of salt and bring to the boil.
Heat the oil with the rice, seasoned with pepper, in another pan over a low heat, stirring frequently, for 5 minutes.
Pour the salted, boiling water over the rice, add the cardamom pods, half-cover the pan and cook over a low heat for 10–12 minutes until all the water has been absorbed. Taste and adjust the seasoning if necessary. Serve hot.

Onion rice

Serves 6
Preparation: 10 minutes
Cooking: 15 minutes

3 cups Thai rice
2 white onions, cut into thin wedges
1 tablespoon olive oil
salt and freshly ground black pepper

Wash the rice in several changes of water until the water runs clear.
Pour 1.5 litres/2½ pints/6 cups water into a pan, add a pinch of salt and bring to the boil.
Heat the oil with the rice and onions, seasoned with pepper, in another pan over a low heat, stirring frequently, for 5 minutes.
Pour the salted, boiling water over the rice, but do not stir. Half-cover the saucepan and cook over a low heat for 10–12 minute until all the water has been absorbed. Taste and adjust the seasoning if necessary. Serve hot.

Saffron rice

Serves 6
Preparation: 5 minutes
Cooking: 15 minutes

3 cups basmati rice
generous pinch of saffron threads
1 tablespoon olive oil
salt and freshly ground black pepper

Wash the rice in several changes of water until the water runs clear.
Pour 1.5 litres/2½ pints/6 cups water into a pan, add the saffron and bring to the boil.
Heat the oil with the rice, seasoned with pepper, in another pan over a low heat, stirring frequently, for 5 minutes.
Pour the boiling, saffron-flavoured water over the rice, but do not stir. Half-cover the saucepan and cook over a low heat for 10–12 minutes until all the water has been absorbed. Taste and adjust the seasoning if necessary. Serve hot.

Glutinous rice

Serves 6
Soaking: 12 hours
Preparation: 5 minutes
Cooking: 1 hour

450 g glutinous rice

Wash the rice in several changes of water until the water runs clear. Place in a bowl, pour in enough water to cover and leave to soak in a cool place for 12 hours.
Drain the rice and place it into the basket of a steamer. Steam for 1 hour. until the rice is translucent and sticky.
Serve as an accompaniment to raw fish or, for example, fish cooked in a coconut milk, ginger or fresh coriander (cilantro) sauce.
If you need to reheat the rice, steam it again; never use the oven or the microwave.

Appendices

Index of recipes

Index of recipes by fish

Shopping

Paint and wallpaper
• Farrow and ball: pages 31, 33, 39, 40, 41, 47, 49, 51, 57, 63, 69 b.r., 73, 77, 79, 83, 89, 90, 119, 121, 123, 137, 145, 147, 159, 151, 169, 171, 173, 175, 179, 181, 183.
AC Matière: page 117, page 149 t.r./b.l., page 165 t.l.

Fabrics and table linen
• Agape: pages 31, 35, 36, 37, 53, 71, 77, 80, 81, 84, 91, 93, 112, 113, 115, 118, 125, 131, 139, 141, 149 t.l., 165 b.r., 183, 185.
Zéro one one: page 35 napkin.
• Jeannine Cros: page 31 t.l. and b.l., tea towel page 37, tea towel page 49 t.r. and b.l., tea towel page 60, page 69 t.l./t.r./b.l., 75, 87, page 135 t.r., 138, 143, 145 b.l., 185 t.r.
Le Bon Marché: page 43.

Crockery and cutlery
• Muji: page 31, plate page 39, bowl page 51, spoon page 55, plate page 87, serving dish page 77 b.r., plate and cutlery page 91, bowl page 115, fork t.l./plate t.r./bowl and fork b.l. page 123, cutlery page 133, plate page 138, bowl page 165 t.r., fork page 165 b.l., serving dish page 155, bowl page 171 t.l., plate page 173 b.r., bowl page 179 t.l., serving dish page 185 t.l.
• Charlotte Vejlo for Luka Luna: cup and saucer page 31 t.r., saucer page 40, saucer page 119, cup page 121, saucer page 125, saucer page 135 t.l., cup and saucer page 165 t.l., cup page 171 t.r., cup and saucer page 179 b.r.
• Agapé: page 31, serving dish and glass b.r. page 33, knife page 35, chopping board page 36, spoon page 37, knife page 40, eggcup page 43, fish kettle and mug b.l. pages 49, 52, 53, serving dish page 55, serving dish page 59, cutlery page 61, bowl and toy boat page 67, serving dish and plates page 69, fork page 70, 73, fork and salt-cellar page 75, serving dish t.l. page 77, spoon page 81, 85, fork page 84, spoon page 89, serving dish page 93, plate and fork page 115, plate t.l. and spoon b.r. page 123, serving dishes t.l./b.r. and bowl b.l. page 131, plate page 133, bowl page 139, serving dish page 141, pan b.l. page 149, 160, pan page 161, 163, funnel page 151 t.r., serving dish and spoon page 175, pestle and mortar page 179 c.r., spoon page 181 b.r., casserole dish page 183 t.l, spoon page 185 t.l., pan page 185 t.r., serving dish page 185 b.l., serving dish page 185 b.r., bowl and spoon page 187 b.l.
• Kitchen Bazaar: plate page 37, serving dish page 51, plate page 89, white container page 135 t.r., fork page 173 b.r., plate page 183 t.r.
• La Samaritaine: glass page 31, glass page 39, fish kettle t.r. page 49, plate page 75, serving dish and knife page 119, plate and glass b.r. page 123, glass page 161, glass and bowl page 179 t.r. and b.l., spoon page 181 t.l, bowl 181 c.r., mug and sieve page 181 b.l., glass and plate page 181 b.r., bowl page 187 t.r.
• Dehillerin: knife page 41.
• Le Bon Marché: plate page 43, plate and bowl page 70, plate page 84, plate page 113, plate b.r. page 165, plate page 165 b.l., serving dish and bowl page 181 t.l. and c.l., bowl page 187 t.l.
• Asa: serving dish page 47, 57, bowl page 59, serving dish page 60, serving dish page 63, plate page 79, pan page 83, plate page 121, serving dish page 165 t.r., bowl page 165 b.l., small dish page 156, plate page 171 b.l., small dish page 175, small dishes page 179 t.r. and c.l.
• Guy Degrenne: cutlery page 49 b.r., plate page 61, spoon page 63, plates page 123 b.l..
• Zéro one one: cutlery page 69 t.r., fork page 113, fork page 118, chopsticks page 123 t.r., chopsticks page 125, cutlery page 185 b.l.
• CFOC: plate page 71, plate page 80, cup page 81, bowl page 131 b.r., bowl page 149 t.l., plate and bowl page 167, plate page 157, plate page 155, plate page 183 b.r.
• Matthieu Beth for Luka Luna: bowl page 90, bowl page 171 b.r.
• The Conran Shop: chopping board and mug page 112, bowl page 181 t.r.
• Stéphane Plassier: serving dish and bowl page 135 t.r., serving dish page 156.
• Tsé Tsé : plate page 143.
• Plein gaz: toy ship page 87.

Address book

AC Matière, decorative panels
184 Quai de Jemmapes, 75010 Paris, France +33 (0)1 42 02 05 16

Agape, vintage tableware
91 Avenue Jean-Baptiste-Clément, 92100 Boulogne, France +33 (0)1 47 12 04 88

Asa
www.asa-selection.com; 00 492 624 189 45

CFOC
167 Bd Saint-Germain, 75006 Paris, France +33 (0)1 45 48 10 31

Dehillerin
18 Rue Coquillère, 75001 Paris, France +33 (0)1 42 36 53 13

Farrow & Ball
www.farrowandball.com

Guy Degrenne
9 Avenue de Niel, 75017 Paris, France +33 (0)1 45 74 01 57

Jeannine Cros
11 Rue d'Assas, 75006 Paris, France +33 (0)1 45 48 00 67

Kitchen Bazaar
11 Avenue du Maine, 75015 Paris, France +33 (0)1 42 22 91 17

La Samaritaine
19 Rue de la Monnaie, 75001 Paris, France +33 (0)1 40 41 20 20

Le Bon Marché
24 Rue de Sèvres, 75007 Paris, France +33 (0)1 44 39 80 00

Luka Luna
77 Rue de la Verrerie, 75004 Paris, France +33 (0)1 48 87 28 18

Muji
47 Rue des Francs-Bourgeois, 75004 Paris, France +33 (0)1 49 96 41 41

Plein Gaz, vintage toys
1 Rue Saint-Benoît, 75006 Paris, France +33 (0)1 42 60 89 57

Stéphane Plassier
sales, +33 (0)1 42 80 07 05

The Conran Shop
www.conran.com

Zero One One
2 Rue Marengo, 75001 Paris, France +33 (0)1 42 27 00 11

Acknowledgements

Above all, thanks go to Manou, to all those who gave their ideas, to all those who divulged their little secrets and recipes, to Brigitte and Paul who gave their advice on fishing, and to David for his sheer talent.

© Marabout (Hachette Livre), 2004
This edition published by Hachette Illustrated UK, Octopus Publishing Group Ltd., 2–4 Heron Quays, London E14 4JP

English translation by Wendy Allatson and Debra Nicol for JMS Books LLP (email: moseleystrachan@aol.com)
Translation © Octopus Publishing Group Ltd.

A CIP catalogue for this book is available from the British Library

ISBN-13: 978-1-84430-141-6

ISBN-10: 1-84430-141-9

Printed in Hong Kong by Toppan